CASES

CASES

HOWARD T. SENZEL

THE VIKING PRESS   NEW YORK

LIBRARY OF CONGRESS CATALOGING IN PUBLICATION DATA
Senzel, Howard.
   Cases.
   1. New York (N.Y.). Criminal Court.   2. Trials—
New York (N.Y.)   I. Title.
KFX2093.S46   345.747′01   82-70132
ISBN 0-670-20603-2   347.47051   AACR2

Printed in the United States of America
Set in CRT Caledonia
Designed by Sharen DuGoff

CHAPTER ONE

1

You have only to walk into a courtroom and breathe of that atmosphere to know what's going on there; human beings smell different when they're in trouble.

The drama in court is greater than in life. It's morally exaggerated, formally overbearing, vengeful, precise, and final. But its depths are invisible, and you can never hear what's going on.

Obscurant information will interfere—shoe dirt, floor wax, ammonia-mop, food and property of the public, perfumed and cigar-scented lawyers, accused bodies that haven't seen a toilet or bath in some time—but you'll know that smell.

And even if you stay there for years and learn to look and listen, induct and deduct, reason and forgive, even if

you ponder and rewrite the experience until it is your own,
even if you grow familiar with it and don't smell anything—it will dominate that landscape.

2

This court is Part AT-1 of the Criminal Court, held in and
for the city and county and the state of New York, in Room
27, and held in a time of declining magnificence, organization, and authority.

The judge looks troubled and impatient. The lawyers
look weary of their smugness. The audience looks taut and
grieved. The defendants are a flow rather than individually
accused personalities. They look like the collapse of Western civilization, manifest in an unending variety of forms.

One after another, the cases are called for arraignment.
They are judged in five minutes or, more often, thirty sec-
onds. They are heard from early in the morning until the
middle of the night, every single day. And still, there is always a crowd of restless cases that have been waiting for
too long.

AT-1 is famous for being a dump and a disgrace, yet it is
the law; as much as any court made up of the rules and
procedures that stand as metaphor for the production of
truth—the living extension of a sacred rite, performed
continuously for over eight hundred years.

From the ceiling, just shy of cathedral height, little
clumps of plaster fall occasionally into the lights and the
proceedings. At the end of each row of the audience,
sleeping policemen rest the pomade or their weary heads
on dark spots in the oak paneling that mark the ghosts of
millions of dollars in police overtime. The velvet rope
guarding access to the court leaks crumbled sponge rubber
where it has split from being overhandled. Thick ridges of
greasy dirt balance on the folds of the limp flag hanging

behind the judge. Above the flag, there is a bullet hole in the wall, right under the *r* of "In God We Trust." The top hinge on one of the swinging doors is cracked. Repeated stiff-arming renders it precarious and exposes a smoky vestibule filled with a float of 250 butts and half a dozen people being told by a uniformed court officer that there is no smoking, no standing allowed. The clock on the wall above them reads twenty minutes past eight; it stopped in May 1978.

The idea that formal human behavior can bring redress for the cruel caprices of nature and the gods is fundamental to social organization in the Western tradition. In the collective conscience, courts, by finding truth, correct wrong acts. The narratives of popular culture bombard the collective conscience with accounts of perfect courts that hear cases of good triumphant and evil banished. In AT-1, justice and its perfect administration is the pursuit, but the fundamentals of social organization in the Western tradition appear to have slipped away. Anything can happen.

Or, as those who know it best say, "You got these constitutional rights over here, but when you in trouble, you in trouble."

<h1 style="text-align:center">3</h1>

It's Monday morning and the court is empty. Most cops have Sunday off, so there are very few arrests. Court is quiet, but the judge is sitting and lawyers are milling beneath him.

Sitting on the prisoner's bench along the side wall is an old black man with a white beard. He looks exhausted, far beyond the signs of the sleep he lost last night while being processed through the system.

A mumble of words and numbers is intoned, and the old man, beckoned by his cop, slowly makes his way across the court. The man is dressed in a long plaid topcoat with a belt and cape sleeves, a worn-out Sherlock Holmes. His skin is dark, African-looking, but matted with a flat gray that comes from sleeping on the street. And he isn't just slow and shuffling. His head never turns, his eyes never blink, and his hands are held too high, as if he has to hear and feel his way, and sneak across the room.

The old man says nothing. His lawyer looks sharp, but all he says is that his client pleads guilty to fraudulent accosting. The judge sentences him to five days in jail, and he leaves as slowly and otherworldly as he arrived, back through the door to the pens.

The defendant is a fake blind man, apprehended while begging, in possession of a white cane and a phony student identification card from New York University. His relationship to his vision is a lot more complicated than a simple fraud, but it's no big deal. He has 104 previous arrests for the same thing.

4

It's late Saturday night. The court has been busy all day—the week's backlog piled on the weekend rush—but by now every case has been arraigned or sent back to jail to appear in the morning. All that remains is a youth. And alone deep in the emptied gallery is his family.

The mother is round and big-bodied, but from the way she holds her head back and looks up through her glasses, you can tell that she is not tall. She is dressed in synthetic medical whites. Maybe she's a nurse, or maybe a cook in a high school cafeteria. Her hair has been hot-combed and wound into a beehive and, since then, unraveled. A plastic drinking straw from McDonald's is stuck through it as a pin. The name tag on her uniform is crooked.

She daubs the tears from her eyes with a balled-up

Kleenex, but, distracted, she misses occasionally and a tear rolls down her cheek. In her free hand, the thumbnail picks the fingernails in rotation.

She keeps putting the strap of her bag back on her shoulder, and it keeps slipping down to her elbow. As she puts it back, she inadvertently kicks the shopping bag at her feet. She leans down to right it, but the shoulder bag slips off. By the time she finds it, her tears are falling on the floor.

Sitting next to her is the father, taller, thinner, with gray sideburns and a mustache. He's dressed in a Gulf Oil gas-station uniform with *Willie* written in script above the pocket, and he's chewing gum with triple intensity. He stretches out his legs and puts his baseball hat into his shirt pocket with one hand, then he takes it out with the other. He bends his knee, but there isn't enough room between the benches to cross his legs, so he holds his knee in his hands for a while, then stretches his legs back and crosses them at the ankle. That doesn't work either.

Beside him sit the kids: teenage daughter with too much rouge, in terror, and the little ones, oblivious and exhausted, passing a cranky, sticky baby back and forth between them. From time to time, the father's arm waves across the kids to silence them, as he strains in vain to hear what is being said in court. When the case is called, they move to a better seat.

Their boy is nineteen years old, tall and thin, small head, and a baby face with heavy eyebrows. If he weren't so tall he could pass for twelve. He wears a powder-blue knit shirt, stiff, flared blue jeans with four-inch turned-up cuffs, and brand-new, clean, low-cut black sneakers.

His upper lip is sweaty and he is shaking, but he rocks back and forth on his heels, sticks out his lower lip, and keeps his arms crossed, looking as tough as he can.

The uniformed court officers yell for him to put his hands down. He closes his eyes for an extended blink and shoves his hands into the front pockets of his jeans. They yell again for him to take his hands out of his pockets. He blinks again and nervously grabs his elbows, then quickly puts his hands behind his back and holds them there. And stops rocking.

The prosecutor says that a monogrammed watch belonging to the victim was found on the defendant. And a loaded .38-caliber pistol. The youth attorney says that the family is prominent in their church and that his client is an A student, with no previous record, and not what he appears to be. The judge asks both lawyers to approach the bench. A conference ensues.

The court employees are in a hurry to go home. They sigh as they watch. The judge holds his head up with one hand. He nods from time to time, but the lawyers are talking mostly to each other. The judge gets halfway out of his chair and wheels it around. Then he gets up completely and stands behind it. Then he paces and sits down again.

The judge rubs his forehead and fiddles with his fountain pen. As the lawyers keep talking, his eyes scan the empty rows of the gallery, growing distant, remote, and impatient.

The prosecutor has to stand on a box to reach the judge. He's only a few years older than the defendant, but he has a suit and a mustache. "Excuse me," his voice squeaks up out of the whispers, "this is a loaded-gun case."

The defense attorney is older and taller. He has a neat beard, a pastel double-knit suit, and a face locked in a grim smile.

Another quarter of an hour passes, the conference breaks, and bail is set quietly. The court reporter couldn't hear it. The judge repeats it, by which time everyone has left.

As the lights are turned out, the family is told that the bail is $5,000. They don't have it. Their boy, their hope, is on his way to jail.

5

The volume of cases in this court is so great that it must move by policy rather than personality; every case must fit the mold. But no two crimes are alike, nor any two cases, and justice demands that each be considered on its own merits, most of which remain unknown to the court and often to the principals involved.

Perceptions rarely intersect in court, intentions never do. When your ass is on the line, you believe whatever you say to save it. As they do, to burn it. This is the essence of adversary proceedings. Coupled with evidence and the rules of procedure, this essence produces the legitimate truth for defining social behavior.

In reality, the court is well aware of its own ignorance and overcome with its futility. The old-timers insist that it used to work years ago. Right here in Room 27, with the same rules, they kept the peace. But not anymore.

When it worked everyone was white. Now it is white men judging black. Because of their own ethnic histories, the professionals who run this court are very sensitive to racial prejudice and obsessed with getting past it to some deeper human truth. There are no overt expressions of racial prejudice in AT-1, but it lies there, like a band of static electricity, crackling when it's least suspected. It's part of the institution, part of America, and not subject to the moral strivings of the personalities involved.

What comes to court is the behavior in the society around it, its political weight and moral values intact. It's the same old system of justice, but it now fails because America is now a failure. America doesn't feel demoralized, it feels exposed as immoral. The agony of how we live and why we act has nothing left to hide behind. The age of innocence is over.

Therefore, after a tradition of progress through illumination, experimentation, study, and reconsideration, and a history of perpetual reform and perfection, the court now clings to the feeling that it is about the same as it was when Druids held it under elm trees.

6

Charles is a tall, slim, black youth. His grandmother was born in Harlem when black people first went there to live. Charles was raised in the public housing projects and poverty that breed crime, and his general opinion of the cases that pass through court is, "Well, let's face it, it could have happened to any one of us."

He insists that he's always been bad, but the evidence is that Charles grew up confident in a life filled with status and reward. His childhood culminated with a basketball scholarship and a college degree in criminal justice. Now he has a little job in court, so he comes to AT-1 to work, instead of under arrest, as his neighbors do.

Charles wears sharp, shiny, flashy clothing and wouldn't be caught in anything washable, because, where he comes from, dry-cleaner clothes are a sign of a steady job and he is thrilled to have one. He wears things like a dark-green shirt with little yellow horses all across it; in each collar he has a gold pin with the same horse, and a matching pendant on a gold chain hanging across his necktie.

Kitty is a small, plump, light-skinned young black woman who also comes from the ghetto and works in court. But while Charles's face is open and expansive and doesn't admit to having known suffering, Kitty boiled her experience into a gruff look and tongue. She keeps a notebook record of what time she punches in and out because she doesn't trust the court's clock. Her general opinion of the quality of justice is a cynical suspiration at the level of naïveté contained in the question.

Whatever it was that brought Kitty to court, alienation

is clearly her path. After graduating from college, she went back to the ghetto and welfare and became the laughing-stock of the neighborhood for having bought the white man's dream of opportunity. It was a while before she got this job, and she is still angry about the wait, although she did use the time to go through bankruptcy and get rid of her student loans. She is very proud of this; the clean slate allowed her to get new furniture, on credit.

Her political position is evident in her eyes, burning through her thick, round glasses. She stated it once: "Honey, I know they brought my great-great-great-grand-mother here in chains, but on payday, that don't bother me as much."

Kitty is best known for her replies: "What you mean you don't remember me? How many five-feet-high overweight black womens work here?" (to a court officer, checking her I.D.). "Get out my face, you little creep" (to a prospective admirer from the legal profession). And "Don't you get on me because everybody knows you don't do nothing but waddle your fat ass up and down the halls, the whole day through" (to a high official in the Office of the District Attorney).

Charles and Kitty are responsible to a supervisor named Vaughan, who is also young and black. Vaughan is from the Bedford-Stuyvesant ghetto in Brooklyn, reputed to be the worst high-crime area in America. Vaughan grew up smart, cocky, and shrewd, headed for a bad end some-where within the criminal justice system. But the system is not just, and it gave him a position instead.

Officer Lockheed has just come out of the Marines. It shows in his posture. He loved the Marines and is happy to have found a job as a uniformed court officer so soon after his tour. Now he can buy the stereo system that he dreamed about in his foxhole in North Carolina. He was too young for Vietnam and is sorry to have missed it. His general view of what happens in AT-1 is that he doesn't give a shit. His style is pure street, but he claims to be from the middle class.

And I work there, too. I started the same job on the same day as Charles and Kitty. Vaughan, with one month's seniority, is my boss too. Officer Lockheed and I were both assigned to AT-1 on the same day.

7

They were all there with degrees and an interest in criminal justice. "Where we grew up," said Kitty, "they be busting so many people, you always knew there were plenty of jobs behind that."

I had no particular sympathy for criminal justice, was white and ten years older than any of them. I had no idea of why I was there, except that I signed up for the Comprehensive Employment and Training Act, and the District Attorney's office picked me.

I didn't plan to stay. I didn't realize that I was too ambitious to accept any responsibility less than glory, and took my safety from an unknown destiny, by hiding out in the last place I would expect to find myself. I didn't appreciate the comfort that came with invisibility. Not until years later.

On first impression, the others thought I was just some old white guy going nowhere. I believed them.

8

"What's the most points you ever scored in a regulation game?" Charles asked the group rhetorically. "My high game was forty-nine points—in college. I bet none of you ever even played in a college game."

"What college?" someone asked.

"Pace. Pace University."

"Where?" said Officer Lockheed. "I never even heard of it."

"Pace is in Pleasantville, New York," I said. "I used to live right near it. Drove past it all the time; it looked pretty nice."

"Yeah," said Charles, "those white boys be okay, sometimes. It's just that beer. Liquor don't do it, but beer, and they get all fired up."

"How's that?" I asked.

"Like sometimes you be going into a party and you hear somebody call out, 'I hope there's no niggers here'; then you know it's time to leave. And one time I was coming back to the dorm and a whole motorcycle gang started chasing me."

"What did you do?" asked Officer Lockheed.

"What could I do?" said Andrew. "I ran."

"Are you serious?" I asked. "In Pleasantville? That's the upper crust of suburban respectability. I can't imagine those things happening in Pleasantville ..."

"Well, they weren't that bad. It's just when they get that beer in them—what it does to them."

"I know there's a difference," I said and fell silent. Not that I felt responsible in any way for what happened to Charles in Pleasantville; nevertheless, being white, I felt a draft and failed to notice that the same wind was powering my invisibility.

9

The job title is Court Part Specialist. For weeks we sat around with no idea of what that meant, and then, after a vigorous afternoon of training, we were sorry to find out.

The court part specialist sits next to the prosecutor in open court, but really works for a computer called the Prosecutor's Management Information System (PROMIS).

For each case, a computer-printed sheet with the name of the defendant, the docket number, the time and place of occurrence, the time and place of arrest, the cop and all his numbers, the charges, and many other bits of information is stapled to the top of the prosecutor's papers. When a case is called, the court part specialist has to tear this sheet off the wad of papers and fill in the date, the courtroom, the lawyer's name, the proceedings, the plea and sentence or the return date and coded reason for adjournment. At the end of the day, these sheets are collected and fed into the computer. When the case next appears, the computer will print it out again, and the court part specialist in that courtroom will record the disposition and then "turn it around" back to the computer, and so on.

The sheet is called a turnaround document. It's all set up with boxes, and all you have to do is check them. In effect, there is no apparent consequence for making a mistake, and no concrete meaning to the work. It could be handled easily by small children or trained pigeons, or chickens. They could punch out the dispositions with their beaks, wouldn't even need ball-point pens.

The court part specialist must also compute the arrest to arraignment time and enter it in a log, which, of course, no winged thing would do.

The court part specialist is the least significant role played within the well of court. It's a brand-new idea with no history, and even for those who do it, it is the smallest and least significant part of their workday experience. The details of the job are not even worth discussing, but the location is prime. No one, without a stake, has ever been allowed to sit so close before.

10

The audience cries and has seizures, foams and sweats and crumbles. People change their seats, rock back and forth, leave and return. They eat and drop crumbs on the floor, already made sticky with spilled soda pop and snacks ground in by jumpy feet. They break their pencils trying to write down a phone number, and tear their pockets trying to get a wallet out. Spectacles slide off sweaty noses, ball-point pens leak through shirtfront pockets, and unlit cigars get snapped off by swinging elbows in the audience.

They signal to their loved ones on the prisoner's bench—the keys, the rent, the love. They are poor people who have lost a child or a breadwinner, and they must wait their day or two, overcome with where they went wrong or where their next meal is coming from.

Polite bums sneak in to fill an empty seat and get warm. Impolite bums and the most crazed of the downtrodden hopeless souls with no place to go come like dying turtles to make one last public nuisance before giving up, and are dragged out screaming.

An old lady sits in the audience holding up a glass star on a string, and turns it, trying to catch the feeble rays of sunlight that make it through the dirty windows. An old man sits nervously on the aisle and flips a neon yo-yo, walking the dog, all lit up. A family huddles transfixed around a jam jar that contains a hairball.

The prisoners are drained, tired and dirty, bleeding and bandaged, or sprinkled with the brown stain of dried blood. Their clothes are torn or missing, their glasses are bent or broken. They shake and shift their weight. They cry and drool, sweat and shiver. They go crazy, are insightful and profound. They become stupid and dumb. They collapse and explode. They hurt.

The prisoners are afraid or angry or guilty or innocent or desperate or down with a bad cold. They are antisocial or social victims. Diabetic, or epileptic, or suffering from heroin withdrawal. They pass so quickly that it's not clear which is which. Blink your eyes and they are gone: bailed, jailed, or paroled, and instantly replaced by the next case.

The lawyers are young, uniformed, bourgeois, careerist, and safely hidden from life in respectable roles. They are the nice Jewish kids I might have been. They are invisible. The judge is just an older, higher lawyer, differing from the crowd beneath him only by style and burden.

The cops are everywhere: snoring and joking in the audience, coming through the door with their prisoners, guarding them, humoring them, beating them. Or sneaking through the proceedings on a shortcut to the tavern, or on a trip to put money into their parking meters. There are policemen in the closet eating hero sandwiches, and on the judge's phone or toilet, just when you need it.

For the most part, the police are tall, overweight, muscular, and pale, but there are plenty of short, skinny, weak, and tanned cops. The older ones sometimes come in suits and ties, and those approaching middle age often wear hippie headbands and brass belt buckles with a marijuana leaf in relief. They cultivate their masculinity with boots, blue jeans, and leather jackets—and lots of jewelry just like the people wear in the ghettos they patrol.

Around their necks they hang their tin: their shield, their badge, their talisman, usually ringed in a black elastic ribbon, in mourning for a brother officer. From their belts, their power hangs right down over the prosecutor's table.

In an environment increasingly made of brittle plastic, hollows replacing solids and artifice for manufacture, the policeman's belt remains to glorify technology and craftsmanship. All is leather, brass, chrome, and nickel-plated, hard, shiny steel. Instruments of torture and death.

High style is two sets of handcuffs worn at each side of the belt, with two rows of a dozen bullets each in leather loops across the back. Or a row of cartridge boxes along the front. Or maybe just a single set of handcuffs at the side, with a chrome flashlight beneath, to aesthetically balance the hanging weapon opposite with a captured flick knife in the top of the holster.

The service revolvers look war-weary, but the personal weapons have handles of carved teak, ivory, and mother-of-pearl. Cops discuss guns as machines, antiques, and in terms of a smart investment in inflationary times, depending on the inherent equity of the weapon. Cops in uniform sit down and place their holsters in their crotches. Cops out of uniform sit down and expose their shoulder holsters, and their little ankle guns, peeking out from beneath their pant legs. Some carry three guns, some carry four. Some even carry five.

11

When court is in session, everyone but the judge and the accused talks constantly to whoever is closest to him, trying to pass the time. Above this hum, it is impossible to hear anything but the endless cries of the court officers.

"Quiet! Let's have some quiet here! Please take your conversations outside, please! No eating in the courtroom! No reading while court is in session! The front row is for police officers only, please find another seat! Take your hat off in the courtroom! Yeah, you! You heard me, mister: Hat! Off! All right, get the hell out of here! Kindly leave the courtroom! No standing allowed! No beverages allowed in the courtroom! In the back there, in the blue jacket, I said, 'No standing.' Now please take a seat! Lady, I told you before, no communicating with the prisoners on the bench!"

And so on.

CHAPTER TWO

1

The purpose of an arraignment is to accuse, and to grade those accused of a crime. The judge functions as an examining magistrate who takes pleas, administers fines and small sentences for specific minor matters, and passes major cases and those who plead not guilty on to court calendars for further litigation. Cases are brought to court by the prosecution, operating through its investigative arm, the police. At arraignment, the prosecution informs the court which cases it cares to pursue.

The prosecution expresses seriousness by presenting a case to the grand jury for indictment, and by requesting high bail. It shows a lack of interest by consenting to parole, or by offering a lesser charge in exchange for a plea of guilty. The value of a case is determined by the quantity and quality of admissible evidence.

The defense gets the facts the prosecution intends to use against it and the defendant's version of them. From this, the defense constructs a scenario more favorable to itself.

The most important part of arraignment is the determination of bail. Everything else is waived, given, or negotiated; a bail application must be argued. A defendant out on bail can be groomed, dressed, rehearsed, and made patient; a defendant in jail is shut off. Also, it is harder to decide to put someone in jail than to keep someone already in there. Defendants held in jail make a worse impression on judges and juries, and get stiffer sentences, than defendants out on bail. It's half their fate, at least.

The sole criterion for the determination of bail is the likelihood of the accused's returning to court. This return is calculated by roots in the community: a job, a family, a stable address—any official connections to respectability that can be verified by a phone call. The seriousness of the charges and the accused's prior criminal record, however, are called valid components.

As a practical matter, almost all cases plead guilty, and most of the rest are not worth taking to trial. Most of the accused have no money, no job, no property, no telephone, and no fixed name or address. No roots but their criminal record, and not much to decide.

But, as a practical matter, jail space is finite and crime abounds. And humanity, in its infinity of selves, is characterized by the magical ability of certain charismatic beings to manipulate those around them and get their will done. The rule of law is very formal and specific, but human magic is always most powerful in relationships that deny it. The sacred cannot be banished, even from AT-1.

2

In the order of arraignment, all logical and emotional values are reversed. The insignificant is often horrifying, while the truly horrible appears quiet and civil. Homicides, for instance, are routine, brief, and calm. The lawyers are waiting to go to trial and won't reveal their plans. And violence is, in general, a cathartic activity. By the time the violent get to court, they are all used up, whereas trespassers who sleep under a roof without permission or authority often arouse outrage and provoke hot constitutional questions. Evil and its story come to court only on paper; the goodness of the revenge is even more abstracted.

Arraignment judges hold the best job in the room, but they are anxious, miserable, and unable to sleep at night, worrying about their performance. Down at the financial and social bottom, the bored daydreaming court mechanics go along easily, masters of their task, and even taking on pretensions.

Court part specialists separate the turnaround document from the prosecutor's papers with a dexterous vengeance that makes it snap through its staples but never tear. Likewise, they snap out of a sound sleep at the setting of an adjourn date and check off the appropriate boxes so fast it looks like a nervous tic. It ain't much, but it is perfected.

3

"Charles, how do you do it?" I called across the elevator on the way down to court. "How do you get here every morning looking so bright and pleased with life?"

"What you want, homeboy?" he said, grinning down at me.

"I want to know how you wake up the way you do. I want to know your secret," I said.

"How I get up? I got to pay the bills. So I have this little clock. I wind it up at night, and when it's time to get up, it rings. And that ring says to me, 'Charlie, you got to pay those bills, get up!' And I get on up. Is that what you meant?"

"I guess so," I said.

"Damn," said Charles. "You're getting to be just like the rest of them. I thought you was a different kind of white— Well, it ain't your fault."

Charles is so literal.

Not Vaughan. Even though Vaughan is a supervisor and earns more, he buys no clothes, has no desire to leave the ghetto, and doesn't like his job.

Kitty resents Vaughan's authority and the fact that he doesn't care about it. She cares about it, and knows, therefore, that she should be the supervisor. She consoles herself by addressing Vaughan with an inventive array of nicknames. She has a gift for graphic one-word rumors.

Vaughan is disappointed by Kitty's attitude. "They made me a little junior overseer, but I'm still on the plantation," he says, "still chopping cotton. And Kitty and them can't see that." But every morning, Vaughan buys her a can of apple juice.

"She needs me," he says. "She feeds off me. So I feed her."

I look to Vaughan for leadership. "What is bail doing in the middle of the notion of equality before the law?" I ask. "Morally, if you've got the money to make bail, it's worse that you did a crime."

"Life was not made for everyone to get over," Vaughan answers. "You're only speaking from the illusions of your privileged upbringing. Maybe it's good for you to sit in AT-1. You think this job is nothing, but it will show you how good you have it. AT-1 is life. Going to jail is part of the black experience. I could go there tomorrow and it wouldn't even bother me. It would be a high school reunion for me, because I'm from Brooklyn. That's how it is. The bail is to make sure they get who they want."

"But that's not right," I say. "And court is the one place where authority must show that it is doing right."

"Well, it's better than when they lynched us."

I pause.

"Then you see what I'm saying," Vaughan continues. "They're going to jail and you're paying your rent. It don't matter to them how you pay your rent, they're still going to jail. And all you got to do is just check off the boxes and bring the turnaround documents upstairs."

I nod.

"Or go out and get a good job and forget about it. Don't pretend you're just some old white guy going nowhere. You got a brain and a mouth and a unique ego and person- ality. And you're white; you can go anywhere you want."

"Yes, I'm white, but I am not so young and ambitious that I can blind myself to what's going on down there."

"Ambitious? You calling me ambitious? Do you know what happened? I volunteered for quality control so I could get upstairs. It's worse upstairs—nothing to do and right under their noses, but I had to get out of the court- room. Once I got up here, they got to know me, and they didn't know anybody else, so they made me supervisor. I didn't want to be no boss, I just had to get out of the court- room. It was bugging me out. Every time they brought a man through in handcuffs, I thought it was me."

4

Vaughan's parents came to New York from rural Virginia. They were childhood friends who lost touch in the great migration following World War II. His father came as an adolescent, part of a family dream. His mother married down South, as a teenager. Three days before her baby was born, her husband was killed in a fight and she ran away to New York City. There, she met Vaughan's father, and they married and had four sons.

Vaughan's father was often out of work and discouraged. When Vaughan was very small, his father went away for a while. Maybe for a short stretch in jail. Vaughan suspects he was a wheelman, but it was never discussed with the children. For a while, the man seemed to give up on life and the whole family worried. The children were raised by their mother, who cleaned house for a Jewish family and somehow made ends meet.

Vaughan's mother was always religious and tried to raise her boys right. She was literate, moral, gracious, polite, and believed in hard work. But her boys grew up in the projects. In the ghetto, the projects are considered lucky homes to get, even if the elevators smell like piss and don't run. The rent is reasonable, they give plenty of light, heat, and repair, and there is a sense of community. People don't move out of the projects until they die, but it's a terrible place to raise children.

For the children, the projects mean growing up under the same roof as hundreds of your peers. So boys, being what they are, fight—individually, and in groups, packs, and gangs—against other projects. It's a primitive world where size is power and nobody avoids encountering all the kinds of self-destructive mischief peddled wherever the poor suffer.

It's as isolated and stable as the medieval village, from Vaughan's description. The heroic figures of his child-hood—the big guy who walked him to school (whom he still calls his protector), the guy whose style he copied in basketball, the guy who turned him on to junk—are all still living in the project, still together, as adults.

"You could almost tell what would happen to a guy by which building he was from. Like, this building be into drugs. And behind that is the refrigerator building. They were into being cool. My building was into basketball, so I got into that."

The boys are all grown up now. Jeff, the half-brother, has been on the same shit job at a hospital for nearly twenty years, but he is happily married and has four children. Dallas, the next oldest, was bright, but he got drafted to Vietnam and came home a terminal nihilist. All he does is think, sleep, and watch war movies. Vaughan came next, the athlete and star. His younger brother Warren was sick as a child and wouldn't go to school. As soon as his mother left for work, he would sneak home. Now he hangs out on the corner, too old to be hanging out, illiterate, confused, and socially disabled. Warren is enrolled in what they call the method for going down, but he's every bit as thoughtful and charming as Vaughan. Arcillius, the baby, is called "Killer." He got the name from his peers at the age of six, when he was the best fighter. Now he's tall and handsome and a ladies' man. He has a little job, but spends too much money on women and clothes, as teenagers do.

Arcillius has two children, as does Vaughan. Warren has one, and Dallas has three.

The boys all grew up to be tall. At six feet, Vaughan is the smallest, but he's been the most recognized. In school, he was put into the fastest tracks and bussed to newly integrated facilities. He liked school, and he liked basketball, and he was very good at both. When he hit junior high school, Vaughan started smoking reefer and quickly went to heroin. By the age of thirteen he was a junkie, and that was the end of books and basketball. Instead, he learned to rob, steal, and hustle drugs.

"In those days, motherhood was still the greatest thing in the world. The baddest stick-up man come over your house, he still paid respect to your mom. And nobody ever robbed old ladies. You couldn't hurt an old lady, in case she was somebody's mother. Not like today, when you can see black children cursing their mother, right on the street.

"We just called it going out. Sometimes we called it making money. We say, like, 'We going out tonight, who got a gun? Nobody? Then we'll go find Big Louis and borrow his.' Then we wait for somebody, sneak up behind them, show 'em the gun, and run with their money."

"Didn't they ever fight back?" I asked.

"Yes. So we got into taking off houses. You know, just the ground floor. It's real easy. People always have suitcases around, so you just fill them up and walk on out. I remember one time though, I stepped out into the hall and three cops were coming down it. And all I could think of was that my mother was going to find out. I got so scared I went right through the window—glass, bars, window frame, everything.

"I didn't think nothing of it then. It's only now that I realize I might have spent the rest of my life in jail for that stuff. I just turned the right corner. It was just luck."

During this phase, Vaughan learned how to dance, how to chase women, and how to talk. And this gave him status and made him proud, and produced his children. He was nicknamed Velocity, and now, he claims, there are a dozen young Velocitys emulating him in the project. And "Velocity" in letters across the brickwork twelve feet high.

"Sex is very important to black men. Maybe too important. Knowing you got to be the stud is some stereotype to carry. And music and dance are very important among your peers. So I practiced. And since I was hustling dope then, you know I was learning how to talk. I mean, when they come back to you all hot because you sold them talcum powder, you got to talk 'em into buying more talcum powder or they gonna try to kill you. So you really talk."

When one of his vital organs finally burst, Vaughan

made it to the operating table less than an hour from
death. Healed and detoxified, he went back to the street
undeterred, but this time with the hustle that would save
him.

He heard about student loans and the open-admissions
policy then in effect at the city university. Doing a little
arithmetic, he figured out that by enrolling he could obtain
a capital base from which to expand his drug business. His
high school career was a junkie's blur—long stretches of
hooky, failures, and a current average of 42—but open ad-
missions meant any high school graduate, and financial aid
was based on need, not merit. After a last semester of fast
talk and performance, they gave him the diploma.

Choosing between his remembered love of mathematics
and criminal justice, Vaughan decided on the more immediately useful knowledge and was admitted. One morning
he awoke from his nod, to find himself a student in a college classroom. He listened to the lecture in amazement.
They weren't much ahead of where he had left off when he
was twelve. He could follow it, and even found it interesting.

He gave up junk, brushed up his reading skills, and
earned a degree in criminal justice, and then another. Before it was over, he had wrestled with Aeschylus, Jean-Paul
Sartre, and the hardest parts of the Western tradition that
he could find. He had to prove to himself that he was as
smart as any white man, but he couldn't believe how easy
it was. He was left with credentials and pride, but also
anger. This was the stuff that they used to fool black people and make them feel inferior, and it wasn't shit. Just a
little con.

And now what should he do?

"I know how lucky I've been. How easy it is for me now.
I want to use my life to help black kids. I don't know how
yet, but I've got to help them. If I don't, then all the luck I
got is wasted."

5

When the bums go back to the park, and the law students and tourists arrive, you know it's spring in Part AT-1. A cold and rainy spring this year, then straight into steaming summer, when the bums return for the air conditioning. But at least it's slow.

A second-story man, retired of course, explains that hot summer nights bring too many people out on the street for crooks to work comfortably. A police officer explains that when it gets too hot, you can't get the cops out of their air-conditioned squad cars for nothing. They say it has always been slow in summer, and used to be a lot slower than this.

The economy is glutted, just starting to pick up the momentum of deceleration. From gasoline to gold, every price has taken on an extra digit. The signs of collapse aren't hanging out yet, but America has begun to feel constrained.

New York City is crumbling ahead of schedule. More dirt and greasy newspapers are blowing in the wind, and the holes in the road are getting big enough to break buses or hide fat fugitives. From the stately heights of old stone buildings, roof tiles and cornices are gently slipping onto the busy streets below, causing two deaths so far this summer. And the mailboxes look forgotten—rusty and without graffiti.

Times are hard; crime is up; court is quiet and cold. Freezing cold. I have to bring a sweater. The President of the United States ordered by decree that, to save energy, all commercial, government, and public buildings must raise their temperatures in summer and lower them in winter. The cold is illegal, but no one knows where the responsibility lies. They think it's somewhere on the night shift, out beyond jurisdiction.

6

In prehistoric times, the site occupied by AT-1 was under water. Later, Indians hunted near it but avoided it. With the coming of the white man, it had dried enough to become a bank above the shallows of a stagnant pond used by the poorest settlers for toilet, drinking water, and the spread of disease. As the city grew, the riffraff gathered there to gamble, argue, and fight.

In 1808, jobless sailors marched there to protest, and the city recognized the location as a trouble spot. The pond was filled in with earth, and a gallows was built, later replaced by a stone courthouse, complete with a jail, a political saloon, and many law offices.

The part of the pond that refused to drain became a residence for the poor, who built over it and called their settlement "Lungblock," in honor of what the air there did to you.

A hundred years later, the city tore down the old stone building and built an enormous streamlined skyscraper, an architectural-masterpiece courthouse, too big for its needs and no expense spared. In 40 years, it was worn out and overcrowded, but it remains in use.

Chiseled into the Indiana limestone walls are unattributed slogans, cribbed from the Founding Fathers: *Only the just man enjoys peace of mind; Every place is safe to him who lives in justice; Be just and fear not; Why should there not be a patient confidence in the ultimate justice of the people?* Across the road: *Good government rests upon the true administration of justice.* A walk around the block and you get the message. It must have been intended to give comfort in the age of innocence, but nobody reads the way they used to.

A gigantic copper-plated aluminum gate three stories high guards the courthouse door. It is perfectly hung, swings at the touch, and the angularity of its design contrasts aesthetically with the curvilinear motifs of masking tape on the glass, holding it together where rocks have come through, until the glazier can catch up with the alienation.

Inside, the lobby is just as tall as the gate. Way up high, where the air is clean and safe, murals depict a thick-necked Hammurabi, Justinian codifying, and Henry II sending out the common law on mighty forearms. Elsewhere on the ceiling, muscular men, sometimes naked, sometimes in police uniforms or business suits, wander in tableaux.

Far beneath, dirt, misery, and noise collect in a crowd of hostility and confrontation. It's a volatile mix.

Prosecutor, judge, prisoner, and public represent four distinct populations that the courthouse must "relate properly, and yet so arrange that no undesirable crossing of traffic ever takes place." Facing east, the right wing of the skyscraper is the prosecutor's office, the left wing the jail and the police station. The courtrooms are in between. The higher up you go, the more important the proceedings get. Halfway up, the building switches from Criminal to Supreme Court. And at the top are judges' chambers, crowned with an immaculate law library, where the loudest noise you hear is the librarian's rubber heels. There, on polished floors and glass-covered tables, legal opinions are researched, written, and perfected, to be dropped on the fray below.

7

The public toilets at the courthouse are very messy. When they are not broken off the wall and lying around in pieces, the urinals and commodes are clogged with butts, ballpoint pens, cellophane wrappers, shoelaces, tissue paper, and worse. Rolls of toilet paper are sunk into the puddles of stale piss and disinfectant. The walls are smeared with human shit, and covered with slogans. WHITE MAN. PINK ALBINO MOTHERFUCKER: GO BACK TO YOUR CAVES IN EUROPE ... I SEE YOUR MAMA SWINING, IN A SWINING PUSSY, LIKE A DIAMOND RING ... OFFICER CULLEY (TPF) IS A LOW-LIFE SCUM BAG. I HOPE HE DROPS DEAD.

Each night, the staff mops to heroic excess, but the traffic is too much.

"Sorry, Mac, you can't go in there, I already cleaned. Didn't you hear me? This toilet is closed until tomorrow, by law," the man with the mop pleaded.

"I'm sorry to fuck you up," said the cop, with his hand edging toward his gun, "but I can't wait any longer. I must go in there and take a crap. Don't try and stop me."

A man, to appear for sentencing, faces jail time; his sweetheart would like to love him good, one last time, to last forever. They sneak into the toilet, where they are arrested under Section 130.38 of the penal code, to wit: consensual sodomy. A Class B misdemeanor.

A private lawyer, finished with his evening cases, strolls with an eye to recreation. "You know I am not a poor man, you should be nice to me," he says to a client-type.

"Well, I don't suck dick for less than forty dollars," she replies. Whereupon they repair to the toilet.

In the judges' chambers, there is a separate room, with a shower, a commode, and a sink, kept highly hygienic. The walls are blank and the door can be locked from the inside. It's clean and quiet, but it's part of the same system. *Out of order,* says a neat note over the sink. *Plumbers have already been called.*

8

It is hot and muggy at sundown. AT-1 declares a brief recess, and the audience flows out into the halls and begins to sweat. Bundled-up bums wipe their foreheads, children whine, and relatives argue. Cops and lawyers tuck in their sticky shirts and yearn for their suburban patios as they suffer to pay for them.

The courtroom across the hall is closing early. Charles is picking the lint off his shiny new suit and stuffing his turn-around documents into a sedate, elegant, legal-looking briefcase that has replaced his gym bag.

As I arrive on the steps to catch the sunset, he joins me, followed by Officer Lockheed.

"What you keep in that bad briefcase there, Charles?"

"These are my papers, Lock. My business," Charles answers.

"What kind of business you got?" Officer Lockheed asks.

"What you think? We just go home after work like a dumb court officer? In this job, we have to take the papers upstairs and do all kinds of things with them before we can leave. Things you wouldn't even understand. Computer things."

"Like what?" asks Officer Lockheed.

Charles winks to me and whispers, "Like drop them off."

"Say what?" says Officer Lockheed.

"Oh, I ain't got time to tell you every little thing I do on this job. I got to get these papers upstairs."

As Charles and I leave the courthouse, we pass a well-groomed young man in a wrinkled suit and dark glasses sitting on the granite steps. His parole slip, all stamped to show the time and place of his next court appearance, is crumpled in his hand. He leans sideways, then falls. Just before his skull smashes on the stone, he catches himself and snaps back upright.

"Oh, my God, did you see that?" I say.

As we watch, the young man does it again. It isn't a miracle, just a loop in a cycle. Charles sneers.

"Young boys throw down their dollars and bet—this time he's gonna fall. But even slick young boys know, a nodding junkie never falls."

Corrected, I remain on the steps while Charles rushes on. The junkie keeps leaning but never falls. The hot wind brings snatches of the cops' conversation.

". . . So I told her, I don't know why you're taking driving lessons, but it's not to drive my car. If you want to drive, you better get your own car. So she went out and got a job, and now she's buying a car . . ."

". . . Are you kidding? Of course I'm out of shape. All cops are out of shape. You try working shifts all around the clock and sitting in the damn car all day long for sixteen years and see what kind of shape you're in.

"You know, I went to high school right around here. I played on the basketball team and finished tenth in my graduating class. Seward Park, what a fucking shit heap that was. I could hardly read and write. What kind of preparation was that to come out in the world and make a buck? I had to become a cop. And they finished me tenth in my class . . ."

Out beyond the cops, young bodies move to the music of their big radios. Spanish boys, dancing too close and too fast for the heat; young mothers, rocking their babies' strollers; hookers waiting for their sisters. All too young and too graceful for this twilight.

Back in the hall, a beautiful young woman in tight short shorts and a skimpy halter struts her stuff across the marble floor and comes over to me. She smiles, then reaches into the halter, takes out her breast, and rubs her hand beneath it until she comes up with a tightly folded note. Leaving herself in disarray, she opens it and holds up a hundred dollar bill.

"Honey, have you got change. I need to make a phone call."

I give her a dime, saying. "You don't have to pay me back," and watch her walk away.

"That's some butt," a voice behind me says. I don't turn.

"I say, she's got a butt, make Campbell's beans forget to fart."

A short bald black man carrying a cane circles and faces me. His teeth are mostly gone. The bandage across his nose is dirty and worked loose from too much talking. It flops like an apron and hides something awful.

"You know, I don't care about sex that much," he says. "Really, I don't."

"It can be a lot of fun," I say neutrally.

"Maybe for a young man, but—excuse me for interrupting—how old are you?"

"I'm thirty-five," I say.

"I'm a good few years ahead of you then, but say you was a young man, say you was about twenty-five years old."

I nod.

"And you came home and found me in bed with your woman, eating her pussy. Your wife's pussy, see. And I'm in there kissing and licking and everything, and you walk in and see us. What would you do?"

"I don't know," I say. "It's a difficult question."

"I know it's a difficult question. That's exactly why I'm bringing it to this point. Remember, this isn't now. This is when you was twenty-five—when you were young and maybe ain't ate that much pussy yet. And you got your pistol on you. You know, you carry it just for protection, but you got it. And your knife, too. And you catch me in your bed, what would you do?"

"I honestly don't know. Nothing like that has ever happened to me," I say.

"Aw, c'mon," he says. "This is your wife's pussy. You know what you'd do."

"Okay," I say, "I'd cut you and shoot you."

"That's right," he says, and laughs so hard he has to hop around the hall to control himself. "That's exactly what he done to me."

9

But there is an order. And if you learn it, you spend more of your time out in the halls, trying to palliate what you cannot help.

"What time was he arrested? Midnight?—then go to room 150 and see if the case has been docketed yet ... Five A.M.?—you're too early, come back to-night ... Monday?—look at the calendar on the wall, she's probably been arraigned already ..."

"If he's seventeen, you'll have to wait for the youth attorney ... I can't give him a message. You'll have to find the arresting officer, he's the only one who knows where he is before arraignment. I know he busted your son's ass, but he's the only one who can ... I'm sorry, you'll just have to be patient ... I'm sorry, the system is all fucked up. I'm sorry ... and please don't call me counselor, I am not a lawyer. I am not a lawyer ... and don't call me a fucking Jew lawyer, I am not a lawyer ..."

Two old men, who the computer said had no previous records, pled guilty to a confidence trick, on the understanding that they would get back the money they were arrested with. One of them poked my chest with his finger: "Hey, man, don't give me that shit. I studied the law. I know it better than you. For six years I had nothing to do but sit in my cell and study the law—And here I plead guilty for a $200 fine. I need my money to pay it. You heard the judge. You can't keep my money. I got my rights!"

A Russian taxi driver, found with heroin in a search

based on a defective taillight, had his hack license vouchered with the property clerk and couldn't work without it.
He crumpled my lapel: "I got wife. I got six children. I
can't work. You destroy me, over what? Little bullshit."

A quiet man bought a stolen watch and was arrested for
it. The case was dismissed, lacking prosecutional merit.
They had nothing on him but his own statement. He was
polite and grateful, glad to be alive and free. But they kept
the watch, and he had paid $25 for it.

I know the order. I try to help, but every time I'm told:
you work for the Office of the District Attorney. The District Attorney does not do social work, the District Attorney prosecutes. Go back to your courtroom immediately.

10

A little man with his head down comes bobbing up the
aisle, determinedly. His glasses sit low on his nose and
show magnified pink where his eyes should be. His nose is
running, and there are little hairs growing out of the top of
his ears. He is carrying a shopping bag in one hand and a
rotting briefcase in the other, held closed with string.

I think he is a member of the audience about to make a
fuss, but as he approaches the well of court, a senior court
officer grabs the velvet rope and holds it open for him.
"Remember, I told you there was one guy you don't stop,
don't ask for an I.D., and don't bother," he says to Officer
Lockheed. "Well, this is the guy. Just let him go wherever
he wants."

"Good morning, your honor," Little Joe shouts across
the proceedings. "Good morning, sir," the judge shouts
back. "Come up." Little Joe wipes his nose, approaches
the bench, and shakes the judge's hand.

"Good morning, Officer," Joe says to the cop on the instant case. "What is this man charged with?"

"Shut up and mind your own business," the officer mumbles. Little Joe walks away, smiling.

"Have a nice day, Officer."

Joe, it turns out, has been coming around since before anyone can remember, creating a little whirlwind of cheer, and disappearing into the pens, where he is given a free lunch, courtesy of the Department of Corrections.

11

Joseph Dunnay was born just before World War I, to a large, poor family in the Jewish slums of Brooklyn. His mother was devoted to and ambitious for her children, and the cultural life of the community was rich. The poverty was rough, but politics and philosophy were rampant and Joe was a curious child. When fistfights broke out at the Yiddish Theater between the realists and the romantics, Joe was there, punching for romance. And likewise at the left-wing bookstores and rallies.

In 1938, when times were at their worst, Joe got a job at Bush Credit Jewelers. The work was packing and running errands, the pay was $12 a week, and the conditions stank. Joe and five other employees held a secret meeting, declared themselves a union, and went off to the CIO to get credentials and advice. But someone squealed to Bush, and before they could call a strike, the company had gone to court to get an injunction against picketing. The union decided to picket anyway, and all were promptly arrested. And found guilty.

Two women were given suspended sentences, but the three men got sixty days in the city jail. In those days, before overcrowding, you got only five days off a month for good behavior. So Joe served fifty days, and it changed his life forever.

As a child, Joe had broken his nose, and it had never healed right. He was left with a deviated septum and a

nasal obstruction which flattened his speech and submerged his voice. But he could breathe, and for a poor
person in the Depression, that was good enough. When he
got to jail, the doctors decided to fix it.

It was a difficult operation, but doctors had a hard time
in the Depression, too, and a job as a jail doctor was a
highly respected position. The Rikers Island prison hospital had excellent doctors. They labored over Joe's nose for
hours on the operating table, then tended him for twenty-
seven days in the hospital and four weeks' recuperation in
his cell. This completed his term, and he was set free, with
nose, face, and passages as good as new. They had given
Joe thousands of dollars' worth of medical expertise, and
he was very grateful.

Joe went back to the jail, armed with fruit, newspapers,
and gifts, to express his appreciation, but he was turned
away and reminded that carrying contraband is a Class D
felony. So he addressed his presents to inmates and guards,
and sent them through the mail.

For the next ten years, he continued to badger the Department of Corrections with treats and supplies—candy,
books, envelopes, pencils, lollipops, and dictionaries. "A
man in jail feels completely cut off from his family and
loved ones. Writing a letter becomes his only link to his
life. Usually, he has never written a letter before and
doesn't know where to begin. A pencil and an envelope
become very important. And a dictionary, especially for
someone who has to look up every single word. And they
don't get any fresh food in jail, so I like to take a piece of
fruit."

The Department of Corrections finally relented and issued Joe a special pass. For the last thirty years, he's been
visiting all the New York jails, remembering the forgotten.

Along the way, Joe picked up the trade of invisible
mending, and earned a living by picking tiny threads out
of cuffs and sleeves and weaving away the tears and ciga-

rette burns in fine men's suits. His brothers all became
wealthy garment manufacturers and looked out for Joe and
their mother. They paid for Joe to take her to Florida
every winter, which he never liked, but did cheerfully as
his duty until she passed away.

When he got older, his eyesight weakened and Joe had
to give up mending. The Department of Corrections took
him on, as a public relations officer, to do what he had
been doing all along.

Now he's getting social security, and rents out a room to
a lodger, which gives him more money than ever before.
He's branched out and now visits Jewish old-age homes as
well as prisons.

"I spend all my time helping people," Joe boasts, never
realizing that it isn't that simple.

Everyone wants to like Little Joe. They're afraid not to,
but he disturbs them, walking around as if he owned the
place, calling lawyers by their last name, opening all the
closed doors and entering the judges' chambers with his
own key. When he insists that 90 percent of the jail population could be released this afternoon with no danger to
the community, if they only had a job and a place to live,
people turn away. And they get nervous when he sits with
a defendant and cries, and then asks the court for parole
into his custody. But somehow they know that in the cynical paradox and sci-fi morality of the system, Joe manages
to be good.

Joe himself doesn't know the secret. "They think I'm a
court buff, or a do-gooder. Which is true. But, really, I'm
sort of an iconoclast."

12

Lockheed, for all his pride in the Marines, has the sheepish
smile of a big kid. He slides through the day, slapping

palms and cheerfully working one-liners off his pervasive needs to hang loose, make love, and play baseball.

As soon as he came on the job, he got engaged. His fiancée is a pre-med student, and Lockheed thinks he ought to be going to night school, since he's going to be married to a doctor. His father, a wholesale brandy merchant, put all his children through private schools. Lockheed is college material, but he's twenty-five years old. This could be his last chance to play ball. And, alas, he wants to be a star.

After a series of quick swings, Officer Lockheed puts down his imaginary bat, strides up to his imaginary home plate, and whispers into the defendant's ear, "Just keep looking straight ahead, mister. Just stare at the flag. You know how many stars is in that flag? Then count 'em. You heard me, mister. You can count to yourself, but I want to hear it."

Then he wanders back and swings again. A little thing he picked up in the service. He'll go far in this system. He's already made his first arrest, heard his name called out in court and everything.

"Yeah, man, I got my first collar!" he said to me. "Right out here in the audience. Guy came into court with a meat cleaver."

"What happened?" I asked.

"It wasn't that big. Legal Aid claimed it was a cheese cutter. They had to dismiss the case because they couldn't show intent. If he had threatened somebody or waved it around, the charges would have stuck. But I didn't know it wasn't a *per se* weapon; it was only my first arrest. Anyway, I got thirteen and a half hours of overtime out of it."

"You mean you kept a guy in jail overnight for a cheese cutter? It's 90 degrees outside, it must be 130 back there."

"One night. Big deal," he said. "The guy was a piece of shit, anyhow."

13

On the seventh floor of the courthouse is a sea of desks that contains the bureaucracy of the prosecutor. The support staff, as they call it. The non-legal aspect. The plantation. Here, those silent and faceless in court are recognized. Here, the precious papers are turned in.

Those sitting at the desks look calm, even listless and lazy, but the dangerous undertow of reorganization lurks. Mysteriously, it moves one desk out of its semiprivate cubicle and puts it in the middle of the sea. It moves another from a blank wall to a window. It shifts this one's executive floor lamp and that one's big ashtray. It replaces only certain of the big green blotters. Here, even paper clips are traded for influence.

The undertow is very esoteric, but behind every desk sits a career and a desire. Real issues like hiring and firing, wages and hours, responsibilities are made somewhere else by tradition and union contract. Little ornaments are the only symbols of success and failure available. And you can only take so much pride in how little you do. The court part specialists who work in court unsupervised are the envy of their desk-bound peers. But the role is no more substantial.

In court, you stand to speak. When a sitting lawyer stands, it shows the court he means to interrupt. And when a standing lawyer sits, it shows he's finished. In court, to stand is to possess the capacity for speech and action. The assistant district attorney always stands—and next to him sits the court part specialist.

The schedules aren't completely rigid, but all the professional jobs rotate, while the clerks, turnkeys, and the guys who mop the floor are all permanent to the court part. Consequently, as each case is called, the DA turns to get his papers and hits the court part specialist on the top of the head with his elbow. The court part specialist usually hollers, which moves the ADA away, but then he's blocking the court reporter, who hollers him back. After a week, they finally learn where to stand, and a new ADA comes in.

As the job wears on, we are all coming to understand in our own way that, as the factory brought drudgery indoors from the fields, so the computer has taken it into the pristine sanctuary of the white-collar sit-down job. There is less penmanship and more poking than was apparent.

"Well, you know they changed the rules when they let us black folks in," Kitty says of her drudgery.

In my wrist, I feel the neck of a fowl.

14

Within the bureaucracy, discipline is maintained by shame. The loss of self-worth is a silent erosion that works its way from what you do to who you are. Unlike the effects of the police function, a social structure built on shame is very stable. Bureaucratic organization has dominated Western civilization ever since the French Revolution. Still, everyone thinks that he can beat it.

If I don't pick up the DA's papers, they bring them out to me. If I fill in my turnarounds incorrectly, they correct them off the court calendars. If I stay at home, they deduct from annual leave. Nothing makes any difference. Of course, there is a limit, but no way to know what it is, or how much of it is your own creation.

I don't even know who the bosses of the district attorney's office are. "Neither do they," said my favorite judge.

It is like being inside a mattress. Wherever you push, the mattress gives, but you're still inside. So you stop pushing and accept that while it molds you, you mold it, and then the only one to blame is yourself.

When they disconnect payday from both one's work and human recognition, they destroy the natural sense of the right to be nurtured by life. Nurture becomes a gift, a whim, or who knows what. Your name is on the paycheck, but instead of pride, you feel dependent and ashamed; and turn to the civil service paper to sign up to take a test for a better job. Thus, the bureaucracy manipulates even the smallest expression of human spirit, allowing ambition to the shy. It's all very civilized.

Every morning at precisely eleven o'clock, it rains toilet paper and hand towels from a window on the fourteenth floor. Some think it's prisoners, others think it's mystical, but I believe it's a civil servant grasping for a human identity.

15

Every other Friday the civil service gets paid. People look a little sharper and act a bit more lively on payday. And everyone is there, even the night shift and those who have called in sick.

Money in the pocket creates amnesia and euphoria. Inflation adds to the pressure, and the streets surrounding the courthouse are covered with hawkers, peddlers, and hustlers. Jewelry, sweaters, radios, tools, used books, drugs, games of chance—anything to get the money off the squares before they even get it home.

Lunch is the celebration. Afterwards, the civil servants struggle back to work, drunk and drugged and loaded up on Chinese food, dragging their packages of latest hit records, small appliances, and discount wine. Often I am right along with them.

It was an hour past lunchtime when I got back, but they hadn't even unlocked the courtroom doors yet. As I waited, Charles came up and put his arm around my neck, roughly. He was drinking from a can in a paper bag, through a straw. Breathing heavily, he dropped the bag and can into the side pocket of my coat and dragged me over to the nearest court officer.

"Officer, this freedom fighter here got a can of intoxicating beverages in his pocket. Arrest him."

The court officer smiled weakly, Charles was all over me again, retrieving his can and bag.

"This right here is illegal," he said pointing at the can.

He burped. "But when you working for the District Attorney, you don't worry about a thing. 'Cause then, you is the law."

CHAPTER THREE

1

How have we come to this? What about the centuries of progress and refinement? And what about the arc of history that bends inevitably toward justice?

Minds may wonder, but this summer legitimacy has ceased to be the central question. The claims of authority no longer rest on a more perfect morality, just tradition and a preponderance of arms.

We are blackmailed by our gasoline; given cancer by our delicacies, our sweets, and our smokes; afraid to walk the streets. The perception of authority in America is becoming grounds for an emotional crisis. We feel betrayed by the strength of our past hope.

The crisis has even curtailed the cherished American limousine. The newspapers covered the wake for the last

19-foot Lincoln to roll off the assembly line. Big shots don't want to be recognized in public anymore.

America has worked hard, gone to school, punched the clock on time, believed in itself, and done what it was told was good. Americans have sacrificed for a future. But after a generation of our most aggressive progress, growth, and reform, we have come to the bottom of a cycle when we were supposed to be at the top.

We the people have lived up to the bargain, but science, government, and industry haven't. The advances they promised are completely out of control. Just when we thought we were getting ready for space travel, there's nothing and nobody left to respect.

"Do the People wish to be heard?" shouted the judge, looking our way. The assistant district attorney had absentmindedly blown his gum into a bubble, which burst while the judge waited.

"Sorry, your honor," said the assistant district attorney, picking the gum off his nose. "At this time, the People serve statement notice, identification notice, and notice of their intention to present this case to the grand jury."

Thus, the feeling in AT-1 that we are not worthy bearers of what this noble institution was.

2

Our legal system began with divine, heroic personalities who revealed, or declared revealed to them, that which was absolute right. Deities are infallible, their punishments appropriate. And when God judged, there were no flukes, no technicalities, and no corruption.

The English refinement of this ancient wisdom was a sophistication called trial by ordeal. The ordeal was a seat dropped into the harbor. The hand of God sank the innocent and floated the guilty up for punishment.

Trial by ordeal is Vaughan's favorite device of all history. That only the pure would be accepted by the water instead of the other way around, he thinks, is the truest expression of the white man's genius. Right up front, it tells you where he's coming from.

Anyway, the Norman conquerors rolled across Britain, cutting, stabbing, subduing, and consolidating the native tribes. The larger political unity they created needed a larger kind of system, and the Normans were obsessed with writing things down and ruling by what was written.

Unlike modern colonization, which cultivates imitation, the Normans tried to preserve the existing inferior systems in the hope of keeping the conquered tribes inferior. But their writings attracted all kinds of ambitious, compulsive personalities who quickly figured out what was at stake.

Soon the mystical charisma of divine heroic personalities waned, and the conquering kingdom overextended itself. A succession of kings were forced to sell off pieces of power to raise cash and armies. The only takers were the aspiring compulsives who knew what they were worth. Soon they had acquired a legal system, for cheap.

In 1215, the Lateran Council suppressed trial by ordeal, and by the end of the century the lawyers had triumphed and modern law began. Same ancient crimes, taxation, and property relations, but now ruled by a new law, obsessed with certainty, uniformity, and simplicity. A law of formal procedures.

The inquisitorial court was replaced by adversarial proceedings, and divinity by a neutral referee. The ancient role of pleader—a friend of the litigant, and guide and aid to the court—was replaced by the attorney. An attorney is a licensed officer of the court who stands in his principal's stead and charges a fee. God had nothing to do with it; just human smarts and the natural buoyancy of truth.

To this day, it remains so, despite the spirit of 1776, the

Bill of Rights, and the landmark decisions cooked up by lawyers to extend their influence and importance that come to us as advancements in liberty. Which they are.

Ever since the Anglo-Saxon tribes regulated the sale of cattle in the presence of a witness and the pursuit of thieves, the exercise of power has been formulated in terms of law. It is our forum of acceptable behavior and has been for a hundred generations. Its history is the history of our civilization. We owe it all to our lawyers—and have they ever collected.

But lately, fading politicians have been able to rally sentiment by saying we are overlawyered and underrepresented. The newspapers are pointing out that twenty years ago there was one lawyer for every 790 citizens, and now there is one for every 470, and why do we need so many? The bleak political sentiment of post-limousine America believes that they are a bunch of cheap crooks. And ancient questions arise.

If the court really is a repository of wisdom seeking to administer justice, why not just have both sides tell their own story in their own words, as they do in Bible stories? Who needs lawyers?

3

Most of the defense lawyers who work in AT-1 are colleagues in the Legal Aid Society. In exchange for a middle-class salary from the state, they defend the poor and indigent. Some are passionate, some ideological, and some are just doing a hard, dull job. But none is like Mr. Dart.

He's average in height and weight, has fair skin, blond hair, and small blue eyes. It's a nordic look, but definitely not Californian. He's intense, and sneers slightly when his face is at rest, but by looks, clothes, and manner you couldn't pick him out of the crowd of nice young lawyers starting their professional careers in AT-1. He's not the crudest or slickest or loudest or most articulate, he's the most opposed.

Mr. Dart hates the system, and the system hates him. Experience and exhaustion usually soften a lawyer with time; Mr. Dart has worked here seven years and grows harder.

He makes his record trembling, spewing citations, insistent; directing the court's attention to this division and that department, wherein they ruled in this paragraph and that subsection. It is all too fast and too loose for arraignments, where there isn't much patience for case law or precedents, but Mr. Dart is determined and radiates disgrace.

Different assistants of the District Attorney identify him with different insects. They say he is dirty and low. Even the Legal Aid crowd often thinks of him, slightingly. And the court part personnel all hate his guts because his cases always seem to run over into lunch and quitting time, when they have plans. Mr. Dart deliberately has his cases called late, they believe, so he can rattle a tired judge and get some bad dude back on the street, wreaking havoc. The judges think he's very smart and worry about him.

Mr. Dart acknowledges the hatred, accepts it, and hates back. He thinks the judges are afraid of him, and he likes that. He has no family, no hobbies, no ideologies, no politics, and no vision of the life to come. He doesn't expect to defeat the system, either. All he has is his law practice, and his anger.

He says he is very clear about whom he is defending and why. He says he knows he has no power, but "if anybody tries to do anything that is not in the best interest of my client, they'll have to pin me to the mat first. That's my job."

He alone will not come to terms with the system or allow its rituals the pretense of dignity. In the eyes of my masters, he is considered Public Enemy #1. And that, in context, steals my high esteem.

"Dart?" the ADA shrieked. "That jerk kept me from indicting by holding the grand jury open so his client could testify and never bringing him in. Kept the whole case from going forward . . ."

"And don't fall for his bullshit. Those cases he cites are usually from Colorado or New Jersey, or some UN protectorate jurisdiction. Last time I had a case with Dart, he cited from a business newsletter published in California. It wasn't even law."

Mr. Dart doesn't want to talk to me because of who I work for. He says the DA's office is one of the most blunt, perverse, brutal, ugly, twisted organizations ever to wield political power. And he says it's getting worse.

"It's an office full of automatons who do exactly as they're told. They're stiff, obedient. They even stand stiff. And you know who tells them what to do—like this new policy of indicting for nonresidential burglaries—those guys belong back in World War II, on the losing side. And that is your office."

I accept that my job will keep me out of heaven, but such is the pace of AT-1 that no one can resist talking to anyone.

"I don't know how you take it," he says. "Only a brutalized, insensitive moron could last on a job, standing around in this monstrous system and not being able to do anything about it. It's nothing personal. I have nothing against you. But, well, I grew up believing that there was right and wrong, and that you did right and not wrong. I thought everyone believed it. If I saw someone beating up someone else, I would try and stop it. And all my clients are down and being beaten, you know.

"It's not that I don't know what goes on here. They could never surprise me again. If the judge pulled out a pistol and shot my client, I would be disappointed and outraged, but I would not be surprised. Not anymore.

"Let me put it this way. The system's notion of equality before the law is like a footrace between a white man and a black man carrying a refrigerator on his back. I just try to get rid of the refrigerator.

"That's all. That's where my anger comes from, and that's where I think I'm effective. I'm not down here to be a figure in a Greek tragedy. I play the game to win, and I do. And that is very gratifying. I was lucky to be born to a family that could afford to send me to law school, and I'm lucky to be down here, doing something meaningful."

Out in the hall, there is a new sign: VICTIMS, WITNESSES AND COMPLAINANTS, PLEASE GO TO ROOM 241. WITNESS AID SERVICE UNIT.

"You see that sign." Mr. Dart points. "The Witness Aid Service Unit is part of the DA's office. Subpoenas are answerable in court, not in Room 241, but defense witnesses will follow that sign, and they will be hidden away by the DA until it's too late to hold a hearing. I mean, that sign is clearly contemptuous. But the DA has political power, so it hangs. As soon as I get time, I've got to sue them over that sign. That's one of the great things about being a lawyer."

4

The assistant district attorneys are lawyers, too. They think I work for them and always want to talk to me. Which is not my job, but every aloofness has a dark underside of sympathy.

In the spirit of fiscal necessity and bureaucratic machismo, the office loads its youngest, newest lawyers with so many cases that they can't keep track of them. They interview the victim, see the harm done from that point of view, and set their hearts on a just conviction. They do not know how routine such horrible cases are, and that the only cases they get are cases the system doesn't care about. So, as their caseloads slip through their fingers, they express the system's desire, and feel it as frustration and failure.

As soon as they understand what's going on and are ready to take responsibility, they don't get assigned to AT-1 any more. In the meantime, they bury themselves in the work and hope they will get promoted to Supreme Court before their egos come apart. That's how they got through college and law school. And now this prestigious job with the New York District Attorney, which is even worse.

In a world of instant gratification gone wild, the lawyer's life is about delay. In an irreligious time, lawyers adhere to an old-time religion. They will put up with anything, as long as success is reserved for the next stage of life. Unfulfilled and trying to get ahead, they defer to their bureau chief, the judge, or some senior partner, never realizing that this is all their profession wants from them.

Nowadays, nearly a quarter of the young lawyers in the prosecutor's office are women, adrift in a bastion of masculine culture. They know how to be, but not who. They flirt with the cops like high school girls, then play hard-ass advocate and absorb the worst. Personal enthusiasm is seen as weakness in women and as strength in men, but always individually, impartially, and nothing to do with sex.

After a while, even the best of them don't sleep nights, but it is not entirely clear that they deserve to.

"It isn't right. It isn't human," I said, half-baiting the ADA. "What's bad and evil only exists on paper down here, while what's present is pitiful and contrite, suffering humanity. How can you stand there and exercise revenge without feeling the wrong? How do you maintain a sense of justice? How do you get through the night?"

"You see," she said patiently, "that's why we were taught to concentrate on the papers and not even look at the defendant. Otherwise, we might be influenced by our sympathies."

She was such a sweet young woman. She sang in the church choir—a good mother, proud of her children, who bettered herself by going to law school. A young black woman, self-made against the odds, who had taken the time from her demanding schedule to explain it to her help.

5

The private lawyer is small and hairless, with large, drooping features. He has a lovely home, family, and reputation somewhere, and a brand-new car in the lot around the block, but he carries no style with him. He could have had a noble face if his life had been different, but too much time spent in AT-1 has marked him. He has a hardness that knows he was intended for something better, and a softness grown from doubtful success.

The private lawyer gets his cases out in the halls, mostly from grieved and guilty parents desperate to do the right thing. They chant "lawyer" and *"abogado"*; whoever answers yes gets their life savings. At least he is a real lawyer.

He insists that crime is caused by human garbage, dumped into this city by Latin America and the Caribbean.

"You didn't see this kind of thing before they came," he says. "The scum."

"But aren't those your clients?" I say. "The people who pay for your living?"

He nods sadly. I hold myself back, then turn and go through the vestibule into court.

He follows. I sit down and take out my library book. He sits down next to me, and reads over my shoulder.

"Frank Kafka. Say, I've heard of him," he says. "What's it about?"

"The system."

"Really," he says. "I bet you know quite a lot about the system yourself. Ever thought of writing about it?"

"Yes," I say.

"You know, when I first came out of college—this was even before I went to law school, must be thirty years ago—I supported myself as a freelance writer. I say supported, I couldn't even pay my rent, but I loved it."

"That's very nice," I say. His face blossoms.

"For the last twelve years I've been working on this book. I showed the first three chapters to a religious publisher, and he was very excited about it. It was incredible, he was really enthusiastic. But that was years ago. The research—the research has taken me so long. I've done the most thorough scholarship. You should see the library I've got—

"But you know, there's no market for this kind of thing anymore. It's all decadence. Culture is gone. There is nobody, really, to appreciate what I've done."

"What have you done?" I ask.

"Well, I've actually proved," he says proudly, "that Jesus Christ never existed."

"Huh."

"The evidence is all circumstantial, I grant you, but it's still a very well-made case."

"But what about these last two thousand years of Christian civilization?"

"Oh, I know the goyim would never accept it. But if you read it, I guarantee you will be convinced."

6

"Deponent is informed by complainant that said defendant did, without permission or authority, remove the electrical meter from the wall of her apartment and throw it out the window."

A complaint from yesterday's cases. A grisly lovers' quarrel made quaint by legalese. Distant, safe, suitable for humor. Adjusted by memory to suit a mask.

Wearing a mask hides and protects and allows the secret self to evaluate and calculate behavior. But masks numb their wearers and cause the anger in the secret self to fester, which causes the real tormentor to grow. Behind every mask, the need to purge accumulates. When the danger is perceived as internal, the flow begins and the secret self empties out. Even what is valuable must go, to be sure the destructive is expelled.

And then what have you got?

Or, as Vaughan likes to ask, "If we are masks with secret selves behind, what is behind the secret self?"

7

The uniformed court officers huddled behind the court clerk's desk. They sipped coffee and chewed sweet rolls, awaiting their call to the fields, when a clerk from the Docket Room came in full of gossip.

"Guess what? You guys are getting Al Taylor back."

"Who?"

"Al Taylor, the court reporter. You know him."

"Nope."

"Sure you do. He worked steady nights for years. Sort of dark-skinned guy with a little 'fro and a bald spot. Kind of crazy."

"Maybe."

"No maybe. You wouldn't forget Al Taylor. I thought everybody knew Al. He's been here as far back as anyone can remember. And always worked night arraignments, right up to this spring, when he had a nervous breakdown or something. All that night court, it's a wonder it took him so long to crack. But now he's coming back to AT-1, so don't say you weren't warned."

"Another nut job; just what we need."

"No. Al Taylor's nothing like that. I guess he was always a psychiatric case, in a way, but he's a great guy. You'll see."

8

The first known use of shorthand was by Xenophon, who used it to take down the memoirs of Socrates. The first general use was by the Romans, who used a system invented by Tiro, Cicero's secretary. In the medieval age, shorthand became associated with witchcraft and magic, and disappeared from polite society.

In the sixteenth century, Timothy Bright invented the first shorthand in English. In the seventeenth century, John Willis invented modern shorthand, and in the eighteenth century there were many successful systems adopted by parliaments, courts, and churches.

With the Industrial Revolution and the rise of business, the Office grew to be an institution, and the shorthands available couldn't keep pace with the demand.

Sir Isaac Pitman, knighted by Queen Victoria for his valiant but failed attempt to reform spelling on phonetic principles, turned to the problem. In 1837, he published *Stenographic Sound-Hand,* a shorthand system based on his beloved phonetics. It proved easy to learn and spread quickly throughout the land.

Fifty years later, a prodigy named John Robert Gregg learned Pitman as a child, devised his own system, and in 1888, at the age of twenty-one, published *Light-Line Phonography* to no success. Everybody was happy with Pitman. Traveling to America, he found the same was true of the big East Coast cities, but beyond them was a vast continent that had never even heard of shorthand. So he crossed the country, preying on fledgling prairie schools and selling them the texts for their new course in shorthand. Gregg caught on.

In 1906, Ward Stone Ireland invented the Stenotype machine. It has twenty-two keys, and any number can be pressed at the same time. It is no faster or more accurate than Tiro, but it is easier to learn.

For the first century of its growth, office work gained status and glamour. Typing and shorthand contests were held; there were reputations and there was fame. The people who practiced these skills had the pride and cockiness of professionals. And then the dictaphone and tape recorder were invented, and something took technology out of the hands of the people and shifted the glamour completely to the machines. Whatever it was, shorthand disappeared into a dumb office job that remains well paid because nobody wants to do it.

Only the court record remains inseparable from its ancient conception.

9

A court of record is one where the acts and judicial proceedings are enrolled for a perpetual memory and testimony, which rolls are called the records of the court and are of such high and supereminent authority that their truth is not to be called into question. It shall be tried by nothing but itself.

When God judged, nothing was written down. Omni-science needs no files. Since the age of lawyers, every-thing that happens in court is an attempt to get the right statements taken down with legal sufficiency, and in the right order. If the court reporter doesn't hear it, it isn't said in court. When a judge tries to shut up a windy lawyer, the lawyer insists that he is making a record. And when the audience asks why they have to keep quiet, the court officers like the answer, Because this is a court of record.

Out of such compulsion, Western civilization has in-herited a series of verbatim agreements that goes back 750 years continuously and contains within it the memory of all that came before. It is one of the biggest projects ever undertaken.

Machines are preferred for such serious responsibility, but there are rules for who makes the record when every-one is talking at once. Machines can hear only the loudest voice; it takes a human presence to hear who is most im-portant.

Fifty years ago, people went to jail for life after crisp three-page trials. Today, it takes several hundred pages just to exhaust the legal remedies. A more thorough truth, but we judge the past by a present we find wanting and as-sume decline.

In ancient times, pleas in court were absolutely formal. They contained sacred words and phrases that had to be pronounced just so. One slip of the tongue and the magical oath was broken. It's the same in AT-1, but where our an-cestors had myth, faith, and the hand of God shaping their exactness, today it is only the overwhelming backlog of ready cases that keeps them saying it the same way over and over.

The job is not what it was. But the medium still draws attention as surely as it did when the conquering Normans instilled their habit of writing what they said, for purgative and power.

10

One morning, in the quiet before court began, Al Taylor appeared. With all eyes on him, he tucked his stenotype machine under his arm and danced, slightly, down the aisle, whistling "Zip-a-Dee-Doo-Dah." With a leap, he crossed the rail and turned serious. He said hello to everyone. And I saw how tired he was.

His bald patch ran from his forehead halfway back. He wore gold-rimmed glasses, a khaki fishing hat, and a wrinkled old fly-front raincoat. Underneath, he wore a velvet jacket—hippie-cut—and a flowered shirt. Below, blue jeans and brand-new Italian loafers, soft, unshiny, light brown.

His clothes dated him, but there was a supple tone to the way he looked and moved. The slight pigeon-toed cast of an athlete, the nervous energy pouring off him—unplaceable, but it spoke of youth.

He unfolded the tripod and screwed his machine to it. He poured ink into its pad and threaded the narrow strip of paper. After that, he read his newspaper and chewed intently through a bag of chocolate brownies he had brought along. People came and talked to him. He looked up from his paper, nodded, and smiled. When he caught me watching him, he smiled at me, too, but he didn't say much.

Before he had finished eating, court began. Two uniformed court officers marched up from the back door, with the judge right behind them. Officer Lockheed went out into the audience and bellowed like an opera singer.

"Hear ye, hear ye, all rise. I said, rise. Everybody up. All persons having business in this court, draw near, give attention, and ye shall be heard. Please put away all newspapers and reading materials. Please cease all conversation. Part AT-1, held in and for the state and the county and the city of New York, is now in session."

"They didn't used to say all that," said the court reporter.

"Give me a break, man. I practiced all week," said Lockheed.

The judge took his seat, all eager and official and obviously new. "What's the matter? Why can't we start? Mr. Bridgeman, please call the first case."

"Sorry, Judge," said Lockheed from the bridge. "We have no ready matters. You can wait out here, or you can go back in the room where you were. It don't make no difference."

The judge fumed. In this overcrowded court, a good judge is one who gets rid of cases before the system drowns in them. At this rate of efficiency, he would never get himself promoted to Supreme Court.

"All right," said the judge, "let the record reflect that it is now ten A.M. I have been waiting in the back since nine-thirty, and I am now informed that there are no ready cases on which to proceed."

"In that case, your honor, the Legal Aid Society would like to make a record," shouted one of it lawyers.

"By all means," said the judge.

"Let the record reflect that it is now ten o'clock and there are three members of the Legal Aid Society present and waiting to interview. There is a basket of papers marked ready, but no prisoners have been brought down from upstairs to the feeder pens."

A corrections officer, passing through on his way to breakfast, stopped to listen. "Hey, I got 160 bodies upstairs and nobody down here. I want this to go on the record for the Department of Corrections. I'm not allowed to go upstairs. It's not my fault."

"Thank you," said the judge.

"The People are ready, your honor," said the ADA.

"Thank you," said the judge again.

The court reporter put down his newspaper, stood up, and stretched. "This is ridiculous," he said. "You are all making speeches for the air. I am not taking any of it down. Nobody has ever ordered the minutes for this kind of stuff, and I'm not wasting my time on it."

Then he covered his machine and walked off, glaring back at the court. "Don't wake me until you've got a row of cases sitting on the bridge, all ready to go."

The judge shouted, but to no effect. A distinguished-looking elderly man wandered in through the vestibule and came down the aisle shouting, "I haven't had a decent night's sleep in nineteen years!"

"Sit down and shut up," said the judge. "Can't you see that we don't even have a court reporter. This court is not in session. If you'll just wait patiently and quietly, I'll answer your question later."

The elderly man sat down and waited for a while, then left. Long after that, the work arrived.

They found the court reporter in a closet full of broken furniture. He was slouched on a three-legged chair, sitting on his heels, with his knees in the air, snoring violently. To wake him the court officer had to pull his arms and legs, shake his feet, and slap him.

Once up, however, he was a true dynamo. "Okay, okay, I'm up. What's wrong with you guys, anyway? Last night I was out real late, and then when I brought this girl home, I realized I had this other girl staying in my bed, so we went downstairs to my other apartment, but her sister was there, which I forgot. So we had to go uptown, and by the time we got there, the sun was up and I just said, 'Baby, I'm too tired. You just get what you can from me, I'm too old to try.' But she wasn't . . .

"Did they start work already? Tell the judge I'm already

there. I just got to make a few phone calls, see if I can get my other apartment back ..."

With the prisoners out and the cases ready, the judge continued to fume and feel thwarted. "Whenever you're ready," he screamed when the court reporter finally strolled back.

The court reporter smiled in agreement, then took a moment to look at the young women lawyers. And then another moment to look at the prostitutes waiting on the prisoner's bench.

"I think I'm going to like working days," he said, finishing his leer.

"Why?" asked the assistant district attorney, who happened to be an extremely attractive woman.

"Well, women look so much brighter in the daylight."

"You mean the lawyers or the hookers?" said the ADA coolly.

"Oh," said the court reporter, pausing for another look, "all of them."

11

The court reporter was born in Bluefield, West Virginia. When he was twelve, his mother walked out on his father and took him with her to a small farm town in Ohio. For high school, he went back to Bluefield.

There he was the star sprinter of the track team, and was voted best dressed, most popular, and most likely to succeed.

After graduation, he joined the Navy and encountered white people and race prejudice for the first time. But he learned to type and got over to the supply corps by transferring himself to NATO headquarters in Paris.

Before the Korean War ended, he was established as ace typist of the command. Al Taylor was brought in to do the typing for all the most important orders because he never made a mistake. He was also established in the households of a string of young French women, where he devoted himself to higher learning. He took his discharge in Paris and carried on for the next six years. Coming back to America saved his life, he says, but it was the worst mistake he ever made.

When he got home, his youth was gone, and he was black in America. Once again, he faced adversity with a hustle. He learned stenotype to add to his typing skills, and took down dictation for hire. It was the heyday of auto insurance lawsuits and there was plenty of work, but they didn't hire black people then.

"I wasn't the first black man to work here as a court reporter. Old Bill came before me. Now he's worth a fortune; he owns the court reporters' school, you know.

"But I was the second. And I practiced until I was the best. I used to drive all over the country winning contests. Honest. Before I took up karate and hurt my hand, I was faster than anybody. And I was doing volunteer work for both the Democrats and the Republicans at the same time. I kept showing them all my awards and certificates, until finally, after they took Old Bill, they had to hire me."

The salary was big money in those days. Enough to put a man on the New York scene. Sports cars, jazz, drugs, wild parties, and sex. And the court reporter was right in the middle of it.

"Was I into jazz? Man, I loaned money to all them cats, even paid Cecil Taylor's rent. And cars? I had the second Corvette Sting Ray in all New York City. Jimi Hendrix got the first one. I'll never forget that car. They used to slash the tires every night because I was living in Little Italy with a white girl. That's where I learned to smile so much."

He took night court, because the action never really

starts before two in the morning, and he gave up sleeping to go to parties and carry on all night long.

Meriwether Lewis went from taking the dictation of Thomas Jefferson to making the great Lewis and Clark expedition. Niccoló Machiavelli went from keeping the minutes of the Florentine republic to writing his famous treatise on statecraft. Al Taylor stayed in criminal court and got known in every high-life night spot.

After a decade of it, the quick-step glide became its opposite. Having avoided every trap and every responsibility, he was trapped in the easy flow of a debt-ridden teenage fantasy, short on cash and youth. The life he had worked so hard for did not contain a future, and the present was dissolving.

Questioning life, Al Taylor limped through a few years of sloppy notes, covered by the bomb explosion that he claimed destroyed them. He made it through a few more years on sheer seniority, then claimed a nervous breakdown and took an indefinite psychiatric leave.

"Three months was all I could afford," he said. "I owe money all over the place. That's the only reason I'm here. I'll never be able to pay off my income tax the way they got me now. I went to them and begged them to put me in jail, but they put a lien on my salary instead. It didn't pay to work for them, so I stayed home. On psychiatric leave.

"I felt a lot better being away from this place. I stayed away as long as I could. It uplifted my mental outlook. Now, I'm even deeper in debt. I had to come back, even for the little bit of money they leave me. I can't get it anywhere else, and I just can't live without it."

"Well, then, you're lucky to have a job to come back to," I said.

"They got you thinking that way already?" he asked. "I'm not lucky. I'm trapped. Take my advice. Get out of here while you can."

Such intense, energetic, restless exhaustion. Sometimes you'd think he was falling apart, had not just come back from a cure. And yet it is easy to see him as a guru.

"Sleep is not necessary at all," he says with a hand flourish. "It's just a mental thing. Mind over body. It's easy, once you learn to do without it. I just sleep to pass the time. I don't need it."

12

If the chaos of court is a symphony, the court record comprises its dance movements.

The dance is centered on the large oak table they call the bridge. In front of it, just beneath the judge and facing the audience stands the bridgeman, with the line of ready cases waiting. Behind it and facing the judge is the cast of characters: the arresting officer stands between the prosecutor and the defendant. The defense attorney stands between the cop and his collar.

It is a bridge in the naval sense of a platform for the officer in command. Lawyers used to pay the bridgeman in order to get their cases called. Nowadays, they're called in order of request, and the bridge is more of a moat.

An arraignment begins when the bridgeman picks up the court papers, turns to the court reporter on his left, and calls the case into the record.

While the other side is making their record, the prosecutor whispers into the ears of the cop at his side, and the defense attorney whispers to the defendant at his. When the record comes to an impasse, the lawyers leave their places and travel to the judge's bench, where they bend in whispered conference.

Anything said in open court is on the record; anything whispered is off. And everyone, at all times, has a loaded gun or a lawyer between him and whomever he would be most likely to strangle.

Every moment has a reason and a history and reveals an order. People move papers, and papers, in triplicate and quadruplicate, move people. Papers are put in the ready basket when their appropriate bodies have been moved from the holding pens upstairs to the feeder pens behind the court. They tell the lawyers to go to the cells and interview. Papers are placed on the bridge when everything is ready. They tell the arresting officer to bring his prisoner into court. And so on.

The trick is not to chart the bureaucratic flow but to hear the music. For there, in the ordered abstraction of rhythm and tone, the true chaos is revealed.

13

Before the record there was just a stream of names and numbers summarizing lives. Not real names, but the kind you give when you're told you are under arrest. Common names, and the frequent Duke Ellingtons, Billy Eckstines, Stevie Wonders, Perry Masons, Cheryl Ladds and Donna Sommerses. Unusual names. Dawn Portable. Sedan Foster. Johnny Too-Bad. Julian Robb, also known as Robb Justice. And, in order of previous arrests: Waldo Emerson, McLester Ballard Timmons, Waldo Emerson Timmons McLeast, turning into a poem what the system regards as his ineffable, effable, effaineffable deep and inscrutable singular name.

D is the defendant. A/O is the arresting officer. P/O is a police officer. LAS is the Legal Aid Society, defense for all but prostitutes, gamblers, dope dealers, and the middle class, who can afford to hire a private attorney, PA. CW is the complaining witness, the victim. UCO is for uniformed court officer.

When you learn to hear the music the form suggests itself plainly, except for the substance wailing from behind
the masks.

14

BRIDGEMAN: Docket Number Y900100, George Abramson,
charged with grand larceny— C'mon, Officer, bring him
right up.

A/O: He's up, but he's Adamson.

BRIDGEMAN: Charged with 155.30, grand larceny, and
165.40, criminal possession of stolen property, on the complaint of Officer Adamson, the 28th Precinct.

A/O: No. Adamson is the defendant. You said Abramson,
but his name is Adamson.

BRIDGEMAN: I did?

A/O: I think so. Now, what's the judge's name?

BRIDGEMAN: Well, what's your name?

A/O: Could you spell it for me?

BRIDGEMAN: Officer!

A/O (*raising his right hand*): I do.

BRIDGEMAN (*shuffling the papers*): Here it is, Smith. On
complaint of Officer Smith, the 28th Precinct.

A/O: No, I'm Smith. I asked you the judge's name.

BRIDGEMAN: Officer, you swear the truth and contents of
the affidavit you signed?

A/O: I already did that.

BENCH: All right, let's go. What's taking so long down
there?

LAS: No trouble, your honor. (*Turning to the prosecutor*)
Petit larceny and time served?

DA: Fine. Let's go.

LAS: Okay, Mr. Abramson. If you admit you did it, they're
willing to let you go home.

D: I did it, but I ain't got no home.

LAS: Well, do you want to go to jail?

D: No.

LAS: Then just answer the DA's questions. It's the best I can do.

DA: At this time the People move to add a charge of 155.25, petit larceny, for purposes of disposition.

LAS: At this time, my client offers to plead guilty to the reduced and added charge. He waives formal arraignment . . .

DA: I'm sorry, but I'll have to arraign.

BENCH: All right.

DA: Sir, is your name George Abramson?

D: No, Adamson.

DA: Mr. Adamson, is that your lawyer standing next to you?

LAS: Say yes.

D: Yes.

DA: Did you discuss the case with him adequately?

D: Yes.

DA: Do you understand that a plea of guilty is the same as a conviction after trial, and that by pleading guilty you give up your right to trial, your right to call witnesses on your own behalf, and your right to cross-examine witnesses brought against you? Do you understand that you are giving up all those rights?

D: Yes.

DA: It is charged that on the night of April 23, on the corner of Broadway, you acted disorderly and took a purse from Viola Simpson. Are the facts true as stated?

D: It wasn't just that.

LAS: Your honor, my client willingly admits his guilt.

BENCH: All right, I'll finish the elocution myself. Mr. Adamson, did you do it?

D: Your honor, I didn't have nothing to eat for two days,

and she was coming out of a restaurant, so I know she just ate. I snatched her purse.

BENCH: And no one threatened you or made any promises to get you to enter this plea?

D: He told me I could go.

BENCH: That's right. The plea is acceptable to the court. Sentence of the court, time served.

BENCH: But the offer is 90 days, only 90 days.

D: I said I won't take more than 60.

BENCH: My God, this is arrogance. A Class A felony drug sale, punishable by a sentence of 15 years to life, and they are offering you a plea to a misdemeanor and 90 days. That's very generous, sir.

D: You offer me 90 days because you ain't got no case. And if you ain't got no case, why can't I go home right now?

LAS: They are not offering to send you home.

D: Hey, you my lawyer, ain't you?

LAS: Yes.

D: Then how come you never talk to me?

LAS: I am trying to determine your circumstances. What you say doesn't mean shit. What matters is what's on the court papers and the record.

D: Well, I want this placed in the papers. It's a medical document. A list of the injuries to me, from arrest.

LAS: I'm sorry, sir. We have no plea.

BENCH: Keep that list, sir. The matter will have to be litigated. Is the District Attorney asking for any bail?

DA: $500.

BENCH: $500 bail.

D: I'll take the 90 days. I'm guilty.

After formal arraignment and sentencing.

BRIDGEMAN: Let the record reflect the defendant is being handed written notice of his right to appeal in English— Hey, man, don't throw that on the floor!—and Spanish, within sixty days.

LAS: Believe me, you did the right thing. I'll explain it later.

D: I don't want to hear it. Get away from me.

BENCH: You know, there are times when a lawyer must take the advice of his client. So long, Counselor.

BRIDGEMAN: Docket Number Y900235, Larry Jones, charged with 165.40, criminal possession of stolen property. Also Docket Number Y861623, Larry Jones, also known as Robert Burns on a warrant. Counselor, waive the reading of the rights and charges?

LAS: So waived.

BRIDGEMAN: Move to vacate the warrant?

LAS: So moved, may we approach the bench?

BENCH: By all means, come up.

DA (after bench conference): Officer, why did you stop him?

A/O: Counselor, he was flagging down taxis in the middle of the road and trying to sell them portable TVs.

DA: He was?

A/O: Yeah. He come over the bridge from Jersey under the impression that if he stole them in another jurisdiction, he couldn't be touched for it here.

LAS: Your honor, at this time, my client pleads guilty as charged.

DA: I'll have to partially arraign. Um, state your name for the record and please speak up so the court reporter can hear you.

D: Ronald Kite.

DA: Are you also known as Robert Burns and Larry Jones?

D: Ronald Kite is my right name.

DA: Did you discuss the case with your lawyer before entering a plea of guilty?

D: Yes.

DA: And do you waive your right to trial and all subsidiary rights therein?

D: Yes.

DA: In the middle of the night, last night at 4 A.M. you were in possession of two stolen television sets?

D: Yes.

DA: How did you know they were stolen?

D: I stole them.

DA: The plea is acceptable to the People.

BENCH: The plea is acceptable to the court. Thirty days' jail, to run concurrent with Y861623.

BRIDGEMAN: You are entitled to free communication by letter or telephone courtesy the Department of Corrections. Officer, lodge your prisoner and come back for your commit.

BRIDGEMAN: Docket Number Y900309, Planet Sledge, charged with 205.30, resisting arrest, on the complaint of Officer East.

LAS: Your honor, I'm not sure what to do with this one. While my client is not entirely lucid, I'm not sure a psychiatric examination would tell us anything—

D: I don't want a psychiatric examination.

BENCH: I don't care what you want, I'm going to order a 730.

BRIDGEMAN: Put your hands at your side, mister, and talk to your lawyer. The judge don't want to hear from you directly.

LAS: Excuse me, your honor, but I don't think there is any need. Mr. Sledge wants to represent himself, it's true, but he is fully aware of the charges against him and capable of assisting in his own defense, and those are the sole criteria.

BENCH: I'll determine that. Now just relax, Mr. Sledge, and answer my questions. You know the charges, do you?

D: I been told.

BENCH: What are they?

D: They say I kicked two cops, which I did not do. All I did was attempt to defend myself when they beat me up.

BENCH: And do you know where you are?

D: I'm in the criminal justice system.

BENCH: Do you know where you live?

D: Yes, I live in a state of peace.

BENCH: What's the address?

D: Everything you say is negative, why?

BENCH: Do you know who I am?

D: No.

BENCH: But you know what I do, you know what my role is?

D: Yes.

BENCH: Is there a name for that role?

D: Yes.

BENCH: What is it?

D: Evil.

BENCH: Psychiatric examination ordered. What's the date? Is it six weeks for a return on a 730?

BRIDGEMAN: How about June 2?

D: Everything I said was positive.

BENCH: Maybe so, but you need medical help. June 2 in AE-3. Next case, please.

BRIDGEMAN: Docket Number NY00321, Hankie O'Connor, charged with 155.25, petit larceny, on the complaint of Special Officer Soap, of Macy's.

BENCH: Youth attorney. Where is the youth attorney?

LAS (*hanging up the phone*): Right here, your honor. This is a simple shoplift. We'll plead to the charge.

BENCH: Good morning, Mr. O'Connor. I haven't seen you since I was sitting in Family Court, several years ago. I see you've grown and that you're keeping well.

LAS: Your honor, I don't see the need for this. We have a plea.

BENCH: Just a moment. Mr. O'Connor, were you ever placed in the Renaissance Orphanage?

D: I don't remember.

BENCH: Well, try to remember.

D: I went through Renaissance.

BENCH: How long were you there?

D: I don't remember.

BENCH: Well, try. Guess if you have to.

D: One night.

BENCH: And were you ever admitted at Croakberg?

D: I don't remember.

BENCH: Please make a guess.

D: I was there one night.

BENCH: And the facility at Ricidiville?

D: Three months.

BENCH: Project Horizon. Veritas program. Disdelphia?

D: All of them, too.

BENCH: Mr. O'Connor, when was the last time you lived with your parents?

D: I don't remember.

BENCH: Well, guess!

D: Seven.

BENCH: Mr. O'Connor, give me your current address.

D: Fuck you, man.

LAS: Just give him your address. You're going to walk out of here.

D: I ain't even talking to you.

BENCH: Counselor, please advise your client of the contempt statutes.

LAS: Ah, um, at this time my client pleads guilty as charged and waives all readings, all adjournments, waives formal arraignment, waives prosecution by misdemeanor information, and stands ready for sentence.

BENCH: Conditional discharge. But I'm making it a condition of the conditional discharge that you stay out of Macy's, understand?

D: I understand.

BENCH: You're sixteen years old now, Mr. O'Connor. It's time to make something of yourself.

BRIDGEMAN: Step over to the lamp and sign for the conditions; let's go.

BRIDGEMAN: Docket Number Y900488, William Washington, charged with robbery in the first degree, 160.15 of the penal code, on complaint of Officer Mendoza. Waive the reading?

LAS: So waived.

BRIDGEMAN: Officer, you swear?

A/O: I do.

DA: The People serving 190.50 (5A), grand jury notice, and 710.30 (1A), identification notice.

BENCH: I'll hear you on bail.

LAS: Your honor, my client strongly maintains his innocence . . .

BENCH: I'll hear from the People first.

DA: This is an extremely strong case of a knife-point robbery of an elderly woman. The defendant has a long and serious record, and we have a strong identification.

LAS: What kind of strong identification, because I see on the complaint that the arrest was made over a week after the incident.

DA: Your honor, the complaining witness recognized the defendant, followed him home, and called the police. We are asking that bail be set in the amount of $3,000.

LAS: Your honor, my client strongly maintains his innocence. He is gainfully employed at the Key Food market. He is married and has two children, and he hasn't been arrested in more than two years. He assures me that he will return to court. He is afraid of losing his job. Maybe he could make a couple hundred dollars, but $3,000 is tantamount to detention.

BENCH: Bail is set in the amount of $1,500 bond, $750 cash alternative. Give me the 180.80 date—seventy-two hours makes it Tuesday.

LAS: Wait a minute, your honor. My client can't make anything like that. Couldn't you set a more reasonable cash alternative, say $250?

BENCH: Counselor, he has been positively identified by an eyewitness, what do you want me to do? Tuesday, April 28.

D: You must hear me, your honor.

BENCH: Opening your mouth will only expose you to further dangers, sir.

D: It's true I got a record. But I've been trying to go straight. I got me this little job at Key Food, and I'm trying. I didn't do nothing to no old lady. I swear it to you. The police come into my house and dragged me out of bed, right in front of my wife and children, and tell me I did this thing, and beat me in the face. I didn't do nothing. When you say it happened, I was at the movies with my family. If you put me in jail, I'm going to lose my job. It ain't much of a job, but it's all I've got. And with a record like mine, I'll never get another job. Now, I got $200 I've saved up. I know it isn't much, but it isn't much of a job. Won't you take that?

BENCH: No.

BRIDGEMAN: Docket Number Y900—

LAS: Wait, we haven't finished. I'd like to place my client's injuries on the record. Let me see, severe contusion around the right eye, four stitches in the lip—

DA: I don't see any stitches.

LAS: Mr. Washington, can you turn out your lip for the DA. He wants to see your stitches.

DA: Okay. Is that all?

LAS: Where else did they beat you?

D: I think they cracked one of my ribs, your honor.

BENCH: All right. So noted. Mark the papers for medical attention and call the next case.

15

I looked up from my work and saw a slight young black woman coming swiftly down the aisle. Her hair was up in elaborate corn rows, and there was a lot of gold suspended on her simple white dress.

Unintimidated, she made straight for Officer Lockheed, who was guarding the rail, and started beating on his chest with both fists, more than was needed to get herself arrested.

Quietly, Officer Lockheed grabbed her around the waist and dragged her carefully back down the aisle. The other uniformed court officers looked the other way. When the woman screamed insults, Officer Lockheed released her fists and clamped his hand over her mouth. "Call me whatever you want, but don't you mention my mother," he said.

"What's going on?" I asked of the clerk's desk.

"That's Lockheed's wife."

"Already," I said.

"Yeah, they're newlyweds."

CHAPTER FOUR

1

A milestone passed: the first time a court part specialist quit. It was the tall, slow-walking Irish kid everybody called John Wayne. And sometimes Duke. He went back to his old job, parking cars for a garage. Apparently, after the boss leaves, he can park the cars freelance and make good money. But it wasn't the money—he didn't like court.

The real John Wayne died only a few weeks earlier. The loss was deeply felt in this system. People here really looked up to him. You can see his influence in the posture of the senior policemen, and in the strut beneath the soft flowing robes of the judges.

But judges want to be wise, not John Waynes. They wear their robes unzipped and frayed; casual, but gracefully machismo. The billowing sleeves slow the marks, stamps, and signatures of speedy dispositions, and it's easy to trip on the hem. But the exercise of authority lies in maximizing distance and personal remoteness, and the robe reveals only the hands, the face, and the status. Ancient covering for an ancient role.

"I didn't wear a robe when I first came here," said Judge Woof. "I thought it was too intimidating. Until Herbie convinced me. What's to stop the defendant from saying, 'Shmuck, who are you to sentence me to 90 days?' When Herbie asked me that, I saw that there is only the robe to show that it's the law speaking."

That's the theory. John Wayne didn't need any theory. Or any covering. It flowed through his veins; made people proud to feel obedient. But there will never be another John Wayne, and parking cars is a better job than court part specialist.

A judge, on the other hand, is still a big deal. When a restaurant or a concert hall gets a reservation for the Honorable So-and-so, they don't think of AT-1. They think of power and wisdom and wealth. They think of status and dignity, just what the judges thought when they were children deciding to go into law.

2

Summer drones on, Western civilization wears thin, and the fake blind man, after regular visits, has suddenly stopped getting arrested.

The dirt of cans, bottle caps, broken glass, and other trash now sticks to the warm soft roads and sinks, for future archaeologists to dig up and understand.

According to the philosophy of history, this sense of twilight is supposed to bring profound moral insight, but beneath the thin veneer of hysteria, the *zeitgeist* has settled for the atavistic throes of business as usual.

3

LAS: Your honor, my client has no history of involvement in any violence, so I'm asking for parole . . .

DA: I'm looking at his rap sheet. I see one . . . two . . . three arrests for assault. No, four.

LAS: Well. By and large, no history of violence.

DA: This defendant is a street-corner marijuana dealer of the "loose joints, loose joints" variety.

LAS: Well, your honor, possession is no longer a crime, and it doesn't just fall off the trees, you know . . .

BENCH: By the way, Counselor, my colleague Herbie wanted me to ask you this: Is it a crime for a poor person to steal from a charity box?

DA: Your honor, I'm afraid that in the church I was raised in, it ranks right up there with cheating at bingo.

BENCH: I'm sorry, I can't put the case on for Friday. The People have reduced the charges to a misdemeanor, and the seventy-two-hour period applies only to felonies, as you know. I'll put it down for Monday.

LAS: But surely, your honor, it was never the intention of the legislature to deprive my client of her liberty for an extra weekend because she only committed a misdemeanor?

BENCH: Please. Don't ask me to pick up the tab for the mental aberrations of the legislature. Monday.

A/O: It can't be Monday. I'm giving blood on Monday.

BENCH: Hmmm . . .

A loud squeak sings from the door.

BENCH: Mr. Bridgeman, get some 3-in-1 oil on the hinges

of that door. Do I have to take care of everything around here?

BRIDGEMAN: Maintenance has already been notified, your honor.

LAS: Well, what are we going to do?

BENCH: I don't know. I can't listen to that all day long. I only took this job so I wouldn't have to struggle with these kinds of problems.

BENCH: I am going to parole you, but you must understand that if you don't return on the assigned date, additional charges will be lodged against you for a crime known as bail jumping, a felony for which there is no defense.

D: Excuse me?

BENCH: You don't come back and you're in a lot of trouble.

BENCH: Counselor, I direct you to develop as much information as you can with regard to your client's matriculation status.

LAS: You direct me . . . say what?

BENCH: Call the school.

4

I was sitting in the little room at the back with the crew, reading the paper and avoiding their conversation, when the judge walked in.

The judge is very learned and theatrically tough on the bench, although somewhat porcine. He always lowers his voice for words like "guilty" and "jail." A rare style, but he is worshipped by cops and court officers for his dirty jokes, his stiffish sentences, and the absolute decorum he imposes on his court. He often orders members of the audience removed and threatens wise-ass defendants with contempt, as if he alone could hold back the tide.

"How's your prostate gland, fellas?" the judge asked,

smiling. Everyone guffawed or smiled back, except for the retired Legal Aid, paying a social call to where he worked for thirty years.

He replied, "Not too good. It took me ten hours to get hard. And by then, I couldn't remember what it was for."

Everyone laughed again.

"You're doing a great job, your honor," said the captain of the court officers. "If they was all like you, we could clean up this city."

The judge shook his head, no. "Shall I give you my impression of this system?" he asked. "We are all a bunch of bums on welfare. We take money from this state and do nothing with it. We do nothing for the quality of life in this society and nothing for the lives of the defendants. All we do is generate paper. A huge pile of paper. Without it, the system would stop. And every twenty years, they throw away the paper and start again.

"Do you know that judges get report cards? They show us how many cases we've disposed of, and how many were placed on future court calendars. They even compute the percentages for us. We are just brutes who must fit into a machine and express its policy."

"That's very insightful," said the captain.

"What are you complaining about," said the retired Legal Aid. "You remember the old days, don't you?"

The judge nodded hesitantly.

"Remember old Sam Liebowitz. Boy, I'll never forget the day he sentenced Jake the Jew Rosenberg to death."

"Before my time," said the judge.

"Jake the Jew was a famous stick-up man. He shot a guy holding up a newspaper shop at a subway station in Brooklyn, and I was working in Brooklyn at the time.

"Liebowitz started out as a big Commie, but by the time they made him a judge, he got real crusty.

"Right after sentencing, the court clerk stood up and

said, 'Your honor, you forgot to say, "May God have mercy on your soul." ' So the judge had the case recalled, and had Jake brought right up to the bench. And he leaned over into his face and shouted, 'Die, ya fuck.' "

5

Judge Woof told me this story: Once there was a judge who insisted on judicial independence. The policy on prostitutes is fines, but he thought prostitution was a terrible thing and deserved jail time. So he insisted on a sentence of no less than 5 days. The first girl refused to plead and was calendared for trial. The rest of the prostitution cases suddenly weren't ready. The chief administrative judge was called. Another courtroom was opened; another judge was brought in. The court clerks diverted all cases to that court. After a while, the audience drifted over. Then the lights were turned off, and the judge was left behind, alone in the dark. So you see, we all have clay feet.

6

"Good morning, Joe," said the judge.

"Good morning, your honor," said Little Joe. "I can't stop, I'm on my way to the prison, to distribute some gifts."

"Well, that bag of yours certainly looks full."

"Yes, your honor. I've got fresh fruit, newspapers, pencils, lollipops, playing cards, Hershey bars, and half a dozen dictionaries. I think I have some handkerchiefs, too."

"Isn't that wonderful," said the judge.

"Yes," said Little Joe. "You see, I have two benefactors now who help support my work. Very generous men. I met them in the joint."

7

The court part specialists, sharing a role, continue to grow more at home and less dependent on one another. They are finding their social scenes in the courtrooms where they work, and their private lives are busy. A steady job has moved them up a class. They are making new life plans and discovering that this salary will never buy a house and car the way it used to, and it's not secure the way it was, but it's something to build on. You can see them gaining confidence and position as their absentee rates soar and productivity rates decline, conforming to the prevailing standards. No one, however, will ever catch up to the court reporter, who is all hooked up with doctor's notes and a psychiatric excuse.

All the big Afro hairdos are gone now, even Vaughan's, which he considered a sign of black nationalism and gave up only for women. The clothes have smartened up, too. Vaughan insists that his are Killer's castoffs and he wears them only because they are free, but we each have individual reasons for what is happening to all of us.

Now that she can afford it, Kitty is thinking about having a beautiful baby, if she can find a man pretty enough to make it.

Meanwhile, she does a lot of reading in court, which no one else is allowed to do. Progressing from the literature of the civil rights movement to gothic romances with increasingly lurid covers, she moves finally to an opaque plastic book jacket, so you can't see what she's reading. But her perspective remains sharp.

"You know, it ain't like this in Russia," Kitty said. "In Russia, you're guilty until proven innocent. You know what that means, don't you?"

"No."

"Means, in Russia, they don't bullshit around. They tell the truth about what's going down."

Charles has announced his engagement, and is promising us all a wedding bash, but we must not mention it to the pretty girls in the typing room and ruin his last chance to play the blade.

Charles's vanity gives Vaughan a chuckle. He is also hanging out in the typing room and figures the girls are flattering Charles just to find out about Vaughan from him. This seems extremely elaborate for truth, but it passes the time between punching in and punching out for the parties concerned.

The emerging focus of Vaughan's life is his family. He's a provider now, and moving to a new apartment with his childhood sweetheart and their child. It's what he's always wanted to do; now he can afford it.

He is also trying to find jobs for his brother Warren, and his cousin.

"This cousin?" I asked. "Does he have any experience?"

"He just come out of jail after doing five years on a murder rap," Vaughan said. "The state lost on final appeal and gave him $30,000 for wrongful imprisonment. So, you know he doesn't want a job, and Warren just wants to hang out with him. He's not a bad guy, but . . .

"What's the matter?" Vaughan said to my surprise. "You think a man is bad just because he killed somebody? Maybe he killed a junkie who was robbing his grandmother."

"But the $30,000?"

"They never recovered the weapon. His cousin threw it in the river," he said, pointing at himself.

"Gee whiz," I said, and touched my forehead as Vaughan burst out laughing.

"You believe anything as long as it comes from the bad, bad ghetto, right?"

"Why not?"

"If it was true, I couldn't tell you about it. You're with the District Attorney."

"So are you," I said.

"Oh, no," said Vaughan. "Now you really believe it, don't you? You know, my cousin won't even step on a roach. Our grandmother lived her whole life in Virginia and never even saw New York, and I'm staying up late messing with these job applications. Would I be doing that for a man worth $30,000?"

"No," I said.

"Damn," he said. "I just realized something. You're the last person around here who still thinks I'm black. Thank you."

By appearances, Vaughan has achieved success. He's over—into the stable, secure clover of white America. And so easily, over such a little task. But something has been left behind, and he thinks it's Vaughan.

"My last job was polishing floors on the midnight shift. Minimum wage, real black work. Meditate and buff, no questions. But I exercised and studied every night at work. And during the day I visited my friends and my aunts. I quit smoking, drinking, numbers, everything. I really had my head together when I was buffing.

"Now I can run this game here with my eyes closed and get my business taken care of at the same time. I can act white with them and make them think I'm smart. But the more I do it, the less of me I am. I walk through the projects with this necktie and I'm invisible. I open my mouth and they don't understand. I'm slipping away from everybody, even my family. I'm not even sure who this person is anymore. All I want to do is something to help my people, but every day goes by and my time never seems to come."

8

Everyone concerned hopes for a good judge, a kind judge, or at least a softie. And the judges hope for confidence in their instincts. But where the human beings within the roles see a confrontation of lives, the system that defines them sees a confrontation of acts. For the accused, the court is deaf; for the judge, it is an opaque agony of lies, tricks, delays, and heartbreaking stories.

No one sees as many arraignments as the judge, or hears the same tall stories as many times, or is less able to distinguish them from the truth.

"The thing about arraignments is concentration," said the handsome young judge, his curls falling to his shoulders as he took off his motorcycle helmet. "Every once in a while, you find yourself spending five to ten minutes deciding something you should have seen instantly. You can tell when it's gone, and without it, you lose the momentum."

"Arraignments is molasses," said my favorite judge. "You can't allow yourself to get compulsive or you're dead. You just have to keep moving."

From the other side of the equation, it's all magic. Judges have their beliefs and reputations, but as they grow and change, exasperation drives them through every attitude along the judicial continuum. So, it's not only who you get but when. What professionals call "depending on which side of the bed the judge got out this morning."

9

BRIDGEMAN: Michael Hairpin, Docket Number Y945600, charged with 140.35, burglar's tools, and 165.40, criminal possession of stolen property. Where is he, Officer?

A/O: You mean the Hell's Angel. He's right here . . . Hey, shut up and get over there.

D: You're the one that's disturbing the peace, kicking me in the goddamn ass on my way through the door.

LAS: Your honor, my client wishes to go *pro se.* I've tried to explain, but he insists.

BENCH: Sir, in all the years I have been on the bench, I have never seen anyone defend themselves intelligently. Won't you reconsider?

D: No, I always take care of my own business. I don't believe in sending someone else.

BENCH: But the law is technical, and without technical training—

D: What's the difference? I'm guilty. I'm pleading guilty.

BENCH: But you may not be technically guilty. You don't even know what you're charged with.

D: Yes, I do. I'm charged with carrying a pick handle and a sack of shit, which I found and don't even know what's in it.

BENCH: No. You're charged with possession of a burglar's tool.

D: Well, is a pick handle a burglar's tool?

BENCH: It is if you can prove the intent to use it to gain access to a premises.

D: And I was just on my way to the ballfield to use it as a bat when I got arrested.

BENCH: Then you're innocent.

D: No, sir. I'm guilty.

BENCH: Well, it isn't the function of this court to determine guilt or innocence, but merely to set bail conditions.

D: Well, you better do it quick, because I'm going right out that window in a minute.

BENCH: That's not very reassuring to the court, sir. Where do you live?

D: In California. I'm staying in Central Park, right across

from the St. Moritz Hotel. I mean, that's where I've been sleeping. I've been trying to get out of New York ever since I arrived, without success.

BENCH: Is there anyone you know that you can stay with until your next court appearance?

D: The last time I saw a friend was when I looked in the mirror.

BENCH: It's my job to decide if you are a good risk to come back, and you are not helping me, sir.

D: Come back? I can't even get out. Why are you worried if I will come back?

BENCH: If I let you go, will you return to court on the adjourn date?

D: Hell, no. I'm heading straight for California and I'm never coming back.

DA: I'm sorry, your honor, but the defendant was found with an ax handle and property belonging to the Transit Authority. We think $1,500 bail is more than reasonable.

D: I wasn't found with nothing. I gave it to him, and he arrested me. And it wasn't no ax handle. It was a pick handle, and I picked it up. And them wires in the bag you call burglar's tools, I don't know if they're for rolling tokens or midnight smokin's. I never even looked in the bag . . . You got the necktie, you got the pen, you're the one with the burglar's tools.

BENCH: Just be quiet and shut up if you know what's good for you.

D: Yes, sir, it would be contemptuous not to. And the way things have been going . . .

BENCH: $500 bail. Tuesday. Notifications?

DA: The People will take care of all notifications.

D: Well, then you can meet me in court, as they say.

BRIDGEMAN: Area-ass, step up here.

A/O: No, it's Ar-e-ar-iss.

BRIDGEMAN: Okay. I'm gonna sound it out, just like they say on Sesame Street—A-rhy-a-ris?

D: Arearis.

LAS: My client, Mr. Ira Aree—well, Ira informs me that this is, in fact, his first conflict with the law. None of the warrants is his, and neither is the criminal history. Further, my client informs me that he has a twin brother named Iram. The names differ only by one letter, and they have the same place and date of birth, so the computer naturally made the mistake of printing out the wrong sheet.

DA: Now wait a minute, this guy's got a prior conviction for homicide.

LAS: He says it's not him. It's his twin brother.

BENCH: Spare me, and execute the warrants.

A/O: I got a bad man here. He's smart and he's reasonable, but he's living on top of a volcano, believe me. I just touched him and he went completely nuts. This is just a little attempted grand larceny auto, but he's fifty-three years old. You should have a look at his sheet.

1939, South Carolina, auto theft. 1941, Trenton, N.J., grand larceny. 1943, U.S. Army, grand larceny. 1947 (age 21) New York City, robbery and assault, sentence 5 years. 1954, New York City, loaded gun, 5 to 10 in Sing Sing. Assault, rape, robbery, and burglary through the next decade, tapering off into auto thefts again. Eighty-seven prior arrests.

BENCH: Mr. Poinsette, I think I remember you. I think I defended you when I was a young Legal Aid attorney. I see your record goes back to 1939, that would be about right.

D: (silent).

BENCH: My name is Irk. Don't you remember me?

The judge looks around the room for verification, but no one looks back. The defendant doesn't even flinch.

BENCH: Very well, Counselor, convey the offer to your client and let him make up his own mind. He knows a lot more about the criminal justice system than you do.

PA: Your honor, my client is fifty-two years old. He has no record and is gainfully employed as a securities lawyer with an income of approximately $6,000 per week—
BENCH: Oh, my God, Sidney! Let the record reflect that the defendant is a personal friend of mine. We went to law school together.

DA: Your honor, this was a vicious armed robbery of a brothel. The co-defendants tied up eight people and locked three others in a closet—
BENCH: Did you say brothel?
DA: Yes. Brothel. A house of prostitution.
BENCH: There's a brothel on the northeast corner of Twenty-first Street? That's right across the street from where I live!
DA: Excuse me, your honor. That's the address of the precinct where the arrest was made. The brothel is on Eighteenth Street.
BENCH: That was my next question: How could a brothel be located in the police station?

LAS: This woman stole food for her children. You're not asking for bail, are you?
DA: I've got to. It's in my papers.
LAS: Are you crazy?
DA: Your honor, this defendant has been arrested ten times in the last two years for the same crime. She has never come back to court, and her record is covered with bench warrants. At least one, I believe, on every case. This shows a total disregard for the law and disrespect for the criminal justice system, and for these reasons, we are asking for $200 bail.

LAS: Your honor, my client is the mother of ten children. They are now in the care of her eldest daughter. My client informs me that they haven't eaten since yesterday, when she went out to get them food and was arrested. Under the circumstances, you cannot keep her in jail. This is petit larceny, it's not even a jail case.

BENCH: Mrs. Johnson, you cannot keep stealing like this. We let you go before, but we cannot keep letting you go. You must give it up.

D: But my babies . . .

BENCH: And you must come back to court. You never return. I'm sorry, but I'm afraid that this time I can't parole you. To do so would condone a mockery.

LAS: What? How can you? May we approach?

During the bench conference the defendant loses composure. She is short, dressed in a housecoat, with her head in a bandanna. Her bulk is unobtrusive until she throws her hands in the air and starts to shake and scream.

D: My babies, my babies, what's going to happen to my babies?

The embarrassed arresting officer doesn't know what to do. He got a call from a supermarket and made the arrest. He tries to grab her elbow, but he cannot keep his grip. The court officers jump into the hysteria, pushing, pulling, and shouting, but no one has the heart to kick or punch a brave mother. The whole group topples into a football pile-up with the defendant near the bottom, still screaming.

BENCH: All right, all right, paroled. The defendant is paroled. But I'm warning you, missus. I'm endorsing the papers, so if you don't come back to court, you get a year in jail. Automatically. And you'll get it the next time you're picked up. Understand.

BRIDGEMAN: Tonia Bicycles, aka Fifi Rodríguez, prostitute. Before the court on a warrant. The defendant was paroled to pay a fine and did not return to court. Warrant ordered by Judge Lynch in AE-7.

The defendant looks like a prostitute. Shapely, but with a big nose, sloppy mouth, and a face covered with bumps and spots. Left alone at the bridge for the bench conference, she begins to quiver and tears run down her face.

D: I ain't no whore (*sob*). I've been straight for three years now. But my husband left me last Tuesday, with no money. And I have a little baby. Please let me go (*sob*). I'll pay the fine. I promise I will. Please don't send me to jail. Please.

LAS: It's true, your honor. She hasn't been arrested in over three years. And this is the only warrant in her history.

BENCH: First warrant, huh? . . . Boy, I'm dying for a cigar . . . All right, young lady, I'm giving you a break. I'm going to parole you. Give me a date.

BRIDGEMAN: July 15.

BENCH: To pay all fines, July 15 in AE-17. Paroled.

As the defendant turns, a wave of cheers and laughter rolls across the audience. She herself is laughing her ass off, shaking her finger back at the judge.

P/OS: Fifi beat the judge. Fucked his head. And fucked him up.

A/O: Wow. That was something.

DA: Well, sir, you sure swallowed that one.

BENCH: Mr. Bridgeman, call the next case . . .

BENCH: And did you have a prescription for it?

D: Shit, man, I know this broad uptown that can write any prescription you want, if that's all this is . . .

BENCH: Miss Acth . . . Miss Acth-ch . . . Let me see, here, A-C-H-C-H-T-L-I-N-G. How do you pronounce that?

D: Shine.

BENCH: Case dismissed for lack of evidence. Go home, son, and be good.

The defendant hitches up his pants, from the bottom of which three glassine bags of a white powdery substance fall.

10

Judges are the system's most loyal employees. They do as they're supposed to, glad to surrender any responsibility that the system and the law will take from them. Getting appointed requires, at the minimum, social access to political power so far above the level of Criminal Court that they are judged only by their peers.

However, America always prefers individual personalities to social problems, so when things go awry in court, judges take the blame. Their metaphor is power, they're the big shots, and the country is in that kind of mood.

Criminals must be paroled when there is no evidence in the case against them. That's the law, but the judge who paroles them will be designated as CRAZED JUDGE LETS MURDERER GO FREE by the time the story hits the national news.

A judgeship is patronage, but it is no longer a good job. By the standards of the legal profession, it is not well paid. Today judges are under such close scrutiny that they're afraid to fix their own parking tickets, which, years ago, no cop would have had the nerve to issue.

Every relationship between judge and defendant is personal, no matter what the law says, because that is the only kind of human relationship there is. Playing favorites is the exercise of power. It is not fun, it is not satisfying, and it is not easy. But it remains a major role in a society increasingly made up of bit parts. And lawyers spend their lives waiting to do something grand.

11

Judge Kay is the son of a black sharecropper in North Carolina. He went to college and studied science, then came to New York and worked for the Department of Health. At the same time, he ran a little shoeshine parlor up in Harlem.

After fifteen years with Health, he quit. The shoeshine parlor had taught him everything he would ever need to know, and he decided to use it. At the age of forty-three, he enrolled in law school.

Early in his career, he was assigned from the state's 18B panel to what became a celebrated murder case. Kay not only won, but on acquittal the judge told the defendant, "You better thank God every day for your lawyer. That was the most brilliant defense I've ever seen." And one of the jurors turned to another and said, "We better remember the name Kay, in case we ever get in trouble."

Twenty years later, they made him a judge, but he still prefers to play the modest sharecropper, drifting along on God's goodness and common sense. When I complain to him about the system, he just blinks and refers to his experiential sacred text.

"Well, we had a snowstorm that went on for two weeks, and nobody was getting their shoes shined. I had five employees to pay, and even my salary at the Health Department couldn't do it. But rather than close up, I took my problem to the problem, don't you know. I told them, 'Boys, I can't pay you.' Oh, they didn't like that at all. Then I put it to them, 'Why lose your money and your jobs and hate me? Why not come up with a solution?'

"And don't you know, one of them thought of galoshes. I bought two dozen pairs of galoshes and we sold them the next day. So I bought ten dozen pairs, and we sold them, too. After that, we made a bundle every time it snowed.

"So you see, we are not only the problem but the solution."

Judge Irk is an extremely cultured man. He's so cultured that he won't allow a television set in his house. He started life as a rich kid with a Wall Street inheritance. Straight from law school, he became a crusading Legal Aid attorney. As the years progressed, he became one of their top trial lawyers, which he loved.

Then he made an offhand remark to a journalist, to the effect that appellate division judges were whores who had become madams. Whatever the exact wording, on publication it created a fuss in the appeals court. Irk became a First Amendment hero, but he had to be taken out of the courtroom and public view. They kicked him upstairs to administration, which he hated. Eventually, he became the head of the Legal Aid Society, which, by tradition, leads to the bench.

Irk came to the job as an enemy of the prosecution, cantankerous, and with a light touch when it came to sentencing. Since then, he has remained an enemy of the prosecution, softened, and begun imposing stiffer sentences.

He can usually cut off a lawyer with one of his sighs. Lately, instead of calling formal recess he just walks off, unescorted, saying, "I'll be in my bungalow, my cabin, or my closet in the back."

Judge Brick comes to work in a Yankee baseball hat and windbreaker, and changes into his legal work clothes in his chambers. They say he is a wonderful man, and you can see that in his face, but since his stroke he needs a heavy cane and doesn't say much. They won't give him a courtroom and he won't retire, so they keep him assigned to a little hearing part and send the hearings elsewhere. He just sits there, looking lost.

Judge Woof was brought in to replace him. At first I couldn't believe how open and optimistic and cheerful he was. No matter what he saw, he just carried on as if all of life were grand and possible. He didn't like disharmony, and wouldn't allow it in his courtroom, but everyone could talk for as long as they wanted. As good as the Constitution itself. And such a large presence—tall, broad-shouldered, big smile, a beard, and loud, checkered suits—that it flowed out into court.

A man dragged screaming before him insisted that he was an innocent tourist from Arizona, where he was losing his job. There was an out-of-country warrant that the judge could do nothing about. But he heard the case with such compassion that when the man was dragged away, he was screaming, "Your honor, it's not your fault. I know you are a good man, but . . ."

The bloom faded. Herbie wised him up, and now he wears a robe. And the earnestness of his expression has been ruined by a nagging backache. The ADAs despise him for being soft. The court reporters dread him because he talks so much. And he's too slow to get a good report card.

Still, he clings to his love of the law and its style. Every chance he gets, he drops a *"curia," "ipso jure,"* or *"nunc pro tunc"* into the record. And for every case that Mr. Dart throws at him, Judge Woof suggests three others that might have been cited, and an appropriate quotation from Oliver Wendell Holmes.

Then there's the black judge who started out as a cop and went to night school. And a Hispanic judge who, according to the son of a former member, once ran with the infamous Turbens—the teenage terrors of Spanish Harlem in the 1940s. He writes thrillers now, and just sold one to Hollywood. And there's an Olympic sprinter and three rabbis, one of whom is also a professional opera singer and the cousin of a former mayor. And another former mayor's daughter. And the congressman's sister. And a former mayor's wife's canasta partner. Although, she has already been promoted to the Supreme Court.

12

Three chapters after the Creation, Cain rose up against his brother Abel and slew him. When the Lord questioned him about it, Cain lied.

The relationship between word and action is a basic power relationship. The work of authority is to convert power into images of strength. Authority is the perception of this strength. Legitimate authority judges and reassures that it knows what those subject do not, and so inspires fear and awe. Because might petrifies the soul, human beings reconstruct authority within their intimate lives, instinctively identifying with the mighty.

Even so, people get into trouble by following their innermost needs and desires. And they get out by guile, charm, calculation, and hiding themselves.

To administer justice, this highly fragile, intimate structure must assume an objective truth, existing as objective historical fact, of which there is no such thing. The definition of an incident and its seriousness—premeditation, intent, force, threat, harm—all depend on the body and soul of the observer.

Once this morality has unraveled in the daylight, there is nothing left for might to do but reduce human beings with souls into inanimate, no-count nouns, to be classified, weighed, timed, and disposed of. This reduction also makes judges into machines and faint echoes of the passions that personal authority once inspired.

The judge's mask is the simple moral desire to do the

right thing. But cases require decision, not response. The
rules and policy shut off response, leaving the pain of responsibility without the means to act responsibly.

As crime ravages the soul of the criminal, so punishment
brutalizes the punisher. To take someone's liberty, you
must give up some of your own.

13

LAS: Good morning, Judge Woof.

BENCH: Good morning, Counselor. How may I be of service today?

LAS: This is a marijuana possession case. In fact, the very
kind of case that the District Attorney of this county calls
press conferences to announce that he isn't going to prosecute.

DA: I'm sorry. This is a sale of drugs to a police officer,
working undercover. The lab report on the pills came back
negative, leaving only the marijuana.

LAS: Simple possession is the only charge.

DA: Well, there is some misunderstanding in my write-up,
but it was a sale, even if not prosecuted as such.

BENCH: None of that concerns us. The matter before me is
simply possession and a defendant, twenty-one years old,
who will have to carry a criminal record for the rest of his
life and whose crime really didn't violate the privacy of
the lifespace of his neighbors. It's more of a personal problem, don't you think?

DA: But, your honor, he sold drugs to the police. If you dismiss this case, you'll be condoning that activity. He's a
drug dealer, a known drug dealer.

LAS: You can't say that. I object. It's unprofessional. Contempt!

BENCH: Counselor, control yourself. The words have not
yet been engraved in stone, have they? Is such an irreme-

dial evil being committed that it can't be corrected by reason in a few more moments?

LAS: The DA's characterization of my client is inappropriate and entirely out of order. If there were a jury here, it would be grounds for a mistrial. And not only is it inadmissible, it is slanderous and punishable in a court of law!

BENCH: You mean, as opposed to this environment?

DA: I should add that the Office of the District Attorney has shown great generosity by not prosecuting this as a felony. If you dismiss it, you are making it impossible for this office to continue this policy.

BENCH: Well, yes, I suppose any act of goodwill risks the possibility of running the well dry and leaving none left for future generations. And you know, Mr. DA, if this were some rural county, pristine and lovely, and filled with abundant calendar space, we might have a chance to examine the possession of marijuana as an antisocial act. But it's not. I am going to adjourn in contemplation of dismissal, pursuant to Section 170.50 of the Criminal Procedure Law.

BRIDGEMAN: Docket Number Y965890, Ella G-a-l-o-p-c-y-z-, ah, z-s-k-y—whatever. Charged with 155.25 and 165.40, petit larceny and criminal possession of stolen property, on complaint of Officer Wiltshire, Transit. Bring her up, and—Jesus Christ, can't you guys bust anyone with a normal name.

BENCH: Mrs. Galop . . . Galopsie-zin-zin-zinsky. May I call you something else?

D: Call me by my maiden name, everyone else does.

BENCH: Yes, what is it?

D: Jackson.

BENCH: Mrs. Jackson, how do you feel?

D: I have felt better.

BENCH: So have I.

Mrs. Galopcyznyzsky is sixty-three, about the same size and age as Judge Irk. Her glasses rest low on her nose, and she looks over them, just slightly annoyed.

LAS: Your honor, I've represented this client on previous occasions. May we step up?

BENCH: You may approach.

The conference is heated. The judge soon throws up his hands and motions everyone back.

BENCH: Counselor, you haven't got the slightest understanding of the function of this court, or the role of the prosecutor within that function. You are bordering on contempt!

DA: I am not being contemptuous, and I'm sorry to appear so, but this woman has twelve outstanding warrants against her, which shows her total disregard for the law. You can't let her go.

BENCH: You want to send her for another psychiatric examination, I bet. She's already had two this year and come back fit both times. What's the use in repeating that? This is not a jail case. Frankly, I don't believe that your office will ever take it to the grand jury.

DA: Your honor, may we approach again?

BENCH: No, I want it all on the record. Now, Mrs. Johnson.

D: Jackson.

BENCH: Yes, sorry. Mrs. Jackson. You have been arrested many times in the last two years, and each time you were paroled and failed to return to court. Now, you cannot keep doing this, but you probably will. And so the District Attorney wants to put you in jail. The District Attorney thinks you're a terrible social menace, you know?

D: No, I didn't.

BENCH: Now, you claim that you're a secret agent for the FBI. Is that correct, Mrs. Jackson?

D: Yes.

BENCH: And the FBI allows you to sneak into the subway

because, well, because how else should a secret agent travel? And they allow you to open women's pocketbooks while you're traveling as their means of paying you. Am I right?

D: Yes.

BENCH: Do you know why they would choose to pay you in such an odd manner?

D: No. I'd prefer they sent me a check.

BENCH: So would I, but I'm going to parole you, Mrs. Jackson, knowing full well that you probably won't return. This will allow the DA's office to draw up another case against you for bail jumping. And then the warrant squad can pull you in again, and valuable time and space can be taken up, all on the theory that you are a danger to society. What do you think of that?

D: Nothing.

BENCH: Very well, paroled. Any date convenient to the officer. I don't think the defendant is coming back.

DA: I object, your honor. If that's how you think, you can't—

BENCH: People's objection noted. Next.

BENCH: Again? How many times have you been before this court? And how many times before me? Don't answer yet, I want you to count for a while.

D: Oh, I guess about . . .

BENCH: And didn't I see you last Saturday, gambling on the corner of Madison and Fifty-fourth Street. And personally tell you to knock it off? And what did you do? You crossed the street and started up again, didn't you?

D: Not exactly . . .

BENCH: Young man, the shadow of your life should stretch before you, not hang over you. You can charm the judges and beat the system, sure. But one day someone will come along who you will not be able to charm. Then you're going to wind up in a box. You understand? I'm talking about life and death . . .

D: Yes.

BENCH: . . . and I'm going to second-call this case so you can decide which.

The defendant is wearing new purple sneakers, a denim jacket, and chrome-plated sunglasses hooked backward on his ears and hanging above his shoulders. Across the back of his jacket it says RUBEN, THE HARLEM DANDY *and beneath that,* SWEETER THAN CANDY. *Breathing heavily and bopping slightly, he knows that he is not in serious trouble. The charges are a gambling fine he did not pay.*

BRIDGEMAN: Move to vacate the warrant?

LAS: So moved. Your honor, my client informs me that he did not return to court to pay his fine because he is a student at Columbia University and was taking his final examinations at the time. Fully aware of his obligation, he was on his way to court to pay the fine yesterday, when he was picked up.

BENCH: My son is a student at Columbia. Exams finished the week of May 25.

D: Damn.

BENCH (*covering eyes with hand*): Give him another month to pay and get him out of my sight. Don't let him open his mouth.

LAS: As you can see, my client is not a menace. It's just that at the time of her arrest she was intoxicated. She assures me that it won't happen again. I'm requesting parole.

BENCH: Does the defendant have shoes?

LAS: Yes, your honor, at her friend's house.

BENCH: And she will agree to give up drinking until this matter is settled?

D: You see, I got this medication from my doctor, and I

didn't realize that I couldn't drink and take the medication at the same time. But I promise I will never take them together again.

BENCH: Which will you give up then, the drinking or the medication?

D: One or the other.

DA: The People ask that as a condition of the conditional discharge, the co-defendants shake hands with the police officer they assaulted and apologize.

BENCH: Why, they lost the fight, didn't they?

DA: But what harm—

BENCH: Absolutely not, I forbid it. Don't be stupid, Counselor.

DA: What do you mean?

BENCH: I mean, what am I supposed to do if they refuse?

BENCH: You're in a courtroom, mister. Get that hat off.

BRIDGEMAN: You heard him. Take it off.

LAS: Your honor, my client informs me that he is wearing a religious hat. And that it would violate his beliefs to take it off.

BENCH: I will not hear any case without proper respect shown.

LAS: Excuse me, your honor, but there have been several appellate division rulings on the wearing of religious hats, and my client is well within his rights to insist—

The defendant shot himself in the head, lived, and was arrested for possession of a loaded weapon.

BENCH: Don't you know enough to take your hat off in a court of law?

LAS: Your honor, my client was shot in the head yesterday. Those are bandages. He can't take them off yet.

BENCH: Oh, I'm terribly sorry.

14

After work and punched out, three court part specialists sat on the courthouse steps shooting the breeze.

"Anything another human can do, I know I can do," said Kitty. "Because I'm human, too. All that can stand in the way is my own doubt."

"But you must recognize your limitations," Vaughan replied. "For instance, I can't swim. I never will. I've always had a thing against deep water. Even as a baby, when my mother washed my hair, I was afraid of drowning. So for me, swimming is out."

"No," said Kitty. "All I can hear is that you haven't learned how to swim. Yet."

A bum approached. He was not completely sober or clean, but he was old, and spoke with a high, soft dignity that slipped right into eye contact.

"I lost Mama last month," he said. "My sister Georgia died, too. And I'm a long way from home. Alabama. I have no money and nowhere to go. And nobody. I just came out the hospital. But Jesus is a sweet one. Won't you pray with me for his help?"

Kitty gave him a dollar. I gave him two quarters. Vaughan scowled. The bum put the money in his pocket and sat down with us. After a bit of silence, he raised his sweatshirt and pointed to his scar. It looked like a foot-long sausage glued across his stomach. Then he showed us his identification bracelet from the Veterans Hospital and a bottle of medicine.

"Oh, it hurt in the hospital. Hurt so bad sometimes . . . I just wanted to die."

"Veterans Hospital," said Vaughan. "You must have been in the service?"

"I came out in 1950. I was a cook in the Army. Did

pretty good. After that, I came to New York and worked as a chef in the Manhattan Central Hotel. Finest hotel in the city. I worked there for twenty-five years. After that, we put Mama in the ground. I was Mama's pet, you know. Mama's gonna come and get me one day, I know it."

"Do you have any income at all, sir?" Kitty asked.

"Hey, there's my uncle," said the bum, pointing across the road. "I haven't seen him in years."

"Any money coming in at all?" Kitty asked again.

"I told you, I'm a cook," he said, and hobbled off.

"You see how anxious he was to discuss his financial picture once he got his wine money off you," Vaughan said.

"Now wait," I said. "The traditional function of charity is to curry the favor of the gods who might be watching and looking for a place to bestow their blessings. It's the giving that counts."

"Well, you know I've got the softest heart on this step," Vaughan said, "but I can't see the good in getting a sick man drunk."

"I don't care," said Kitty. "I'm just treating people the way I want to be treated. I got a job and money and everything now, but you never know when I'll be needing a dollar. That's why I give it."

"And what if you're wrong, Vaughan?" I asked. "What if he is the one-in-a-million bum of sincerity. What if it were you, ill and ruined, and your fellow man wouldn't even give you a little chump change to eat on?"

"I've seen enough people with alcohol problems to know where that money is going."

Suddenly he was back, with his uncle.

"This here is my Uncle Breem," he said.

"I ain't your uncle," said the uncle.

"Really, he's my cousin."

"I ain't no kin to you at all."

Handshakes were exchanged all around.

"Just like that bird over there, flying away, I'm gonna fly away when Mama comes to get me. That's how I imagine it. I'd rather be dead."

"I can't understand how anyone would rather be dead," said Breem.

"I wanted to be dead in the hospital, just to avoid the pain."

"Oh," said Breem. "I never had much of that."

At which point, a third, unidentified bum arrived, and the court part specialists decided it was time to go home.

"Don't leave without some advice," said our bum. "Never get married."

"Why not?" asked Vaughan.

"I don't know," said our bum. "I just said it. I got married when I was in the Army. I was a sergeant, cooking and doing pretty good. I met this woman. First night I met her, she give me some trim. It was real nice. Two weeks later we got married. All the time I was in the Army she wrote me love letters, but as soon as I came out, she left me. That's when I came to New York."

We said goodbye and headed for the subway.

"Damn. That's really something," said Vaughan when we were out of sight. "Getting married two weeks after they met. And then, I got the feeling, his whole life went downhill from there. But thirty years later, he still loves her. That's the real thing, poor guy."

As we walked, the unidentified third bum overtook us on the sidewalk and turned left, into the liquor store ahead. Sticking out of his fist were two quarters and the bottom half of a sum of U.S. currency, in plain view.

"Hey, Kitty," Vaughan said, giggling, "there goes your dollar."

CHAPTER FIVE

1

On the fiftieth anniversary of Black Tuesday—the day the New York Stock Exchange collapsed—I detoured down Wall Street on my way to work. There, as advertised, was a street full of American dissidents protesting against the nuclear-power industry. At first, it looked as if time had turned back a generation, to the denouncing of the war in Vietnam. The hair, boots, soft flannel, and denim were the same, but we never had such rosy cheeks.

These were exasperated rustics of all ages, who lived in the woods, where they weathered quiet, simple lives, freed from the manipulations and warped ambitions of big-city success. Until they noticed a dangerous nuclear reactor going up in a meadow formerly filled with daffodils.

They chanted and sang solemnly. In cadres and contact, arms linked; calculated, efficient. They spoke of some nightsticking and hair-pulling by the cops in the early-morning darkness before the TV crews arrived, but very few arrests. They were ready for that too, and determined, right down to the lawyer's phone number written on their arms in ball-point pen. The confrontation, they said, was scheduled for noon.

I didn't stay long. I didn't mind being out of place in a necktie. I didn't mind their ideology. Styles change. But they were chanting and carrying on for life and hope—they were in the world acting right, from conscience. And in the same world, I was on my way to work.

At the courthouse, the specter of radioactive death clouds interested no one. It was the least of their problems, they felt. Let the white man worry about dangers you cannot see, touch, taste, smell, or hear.

AT-1 was empty. The cops had been on demonstration duty, not out making arrests. But in the judges' room at the back—the Hy Solniker Memorial Room, in honor of the fastest arraignments judge who ever lived—big shots gathered and formulated the system's policy. Actually, no one knew what they were doing there, but Mr. Dart assured me that their only consideration was, as always, the media, and that they were working out a way to soft-pedal the anti-nuke story.

At lunchtime, I went back to Wall Street and sat down in the middle of the road, joining the demonstration. Encircling us was a thick wall of cops. Half of them were in riot gear, and the other half were all distinguished old men with white hair, wearing dressy uniforms with lots of medals, and patent-leather shoes. The top brass was out in force.

Suddenly a big blue and white police truck came flying toward the crowd with flashing lights and a wailing siren. The people in the street didn't even try to get out of the way. No one gave. Hearts froze.

Just in time, a trio of high-ranking police officials rushed the truck, waved it down, and made it back up. Then they shut the engine off and took the keys. Three giant cops got out and waded into the crowd. They looked familiar.

As they came closer, I could see how much they were enjoying themselves, flexing inside their leather jackets, swaggering, and twirling their clubs, with all eyes on them. It was Wazlowski, Curillo, and Paprika, three AT-1 regulars from the busy midtown precinct.

When they kept coming, I didn't know what to do. I hid my face in the lapel of my coat, waiting for them to pass. A powerful arm grabbed my collar and pulled me upright. I lifted my head. Wazlowski's face was right in front of my nose.

"This one right here is a troublemaker," he said to the other two.

He was still holding my coat. My armpits were tingling. I threw my hands up and pleaded, "It's me, Howard. From AT-1."

Wazlowski put me down and mumbled. He was not some sadist but a friend who thought I could take a joke. "I was just kidding," he said, crestfallen. "We would never have brung you in."

I felt awful, but it was too late.

A loud whistle blew, the news cameras rolled, and they started making arrests. Working in teams, the cops lifted the passive bodies of the protesters onto hospital stretchers and carried them to the jail bus, under the watchful eyes of their superiors, who grabbed an elbow here and there to adjust the roughness, and called out *Miranda* warnings to the limp en route. No skull-splitting or ass-kicking for the national TV audience, but each and every one a text-book-perfect arrest. The NYPD could demonstrate, too.

I went back to work. By late afternoon, the paperwork began to pile up, in anticipation, as did the politics. "You know, they have an excellent school system down there at

Three Mile Island," a cop told me, "and the taxes are low, too. The nuclear power plant pays for the whole thing. It's a wonderful setup." And an ADA likened the demonstrators to the ignorants who protested against the steam engine as an ungodly union of fire and water. "You can't stop progress," he said.

Of the thousand arrests made on Wall Street, only the 295 who refused to give a name and address were brought in. All the rest were issued appearance tickets, returnable next week. Those detained could be disposed of in one night. Had to be, in fact. Orders from above.

Night court opened early. White faces filled the audience, with three times as many out in the halls. A special heavy-duty, manic Supreme Court judge was brought in. He was freshly shaven, with perfectly combed wet hair, looking his Sunday best. He opened court by lighting a cigar.

"I don't have any investments in Wall Street, and neither does this court," he said. "We are firmly in agreement with your right to express your views and, in this case, firmly in agreement with those views. But there is nothing we can do about nuclear power here tonight. So I don't want any outbursts or other expressions of political beliefs in this court."

It felt like a church.

The first defendant gave a name and address and was given an adjournment in contemplation of dismissal—stay out of trouble for six months and the case will be automatically dismissed. The second case refused. The judge insisted that he give a name and fumed and shouted for a while, but the defendant just shook his head no and remained silent. The judge badgered some more, but to no avail. Then he looked at his watch and dismissed the case.

The excitement was over; the policy clear. To hell with the fingerprints. This traffic problem brought from Wall

Street to the courts would not be passed on to the Department of Corrections. By closing time, they had cleared the calendar and even held a few trials.

BENCH: All right, all right, pipe down. You have the right to a speedy trial, and the right to represent yourself, and you're getting them both right now. Mr. DA, call your first witness.

DA: Officer.

BRIDGEMAN: You swear to tell the truth, the whole truth, and nothing but the truth, so help you God?

A/O: I do.

DA: Tell us what happened.

A/O: He was seated in the street, a public thoroughfare, and I told him to move or he would be arrested. He refused. I told him he was under arrest. After reading him his rights, we put him on a stretcher and carried him to the bus. That's about it.

DA: The prosecution rests.

BENCH: Do you wish to cross-examine, sir?

D: No.

BENCH: Do you want to call any witnesses?

D: No.

BENCH: Do you want to testify on your own behalf?

D: Yes.

BENCH: Then raise your right hand and swear—

D: I'm sorry, I can't do that.

BENCH: If you don't swear, you can't testify.

D: Okay.

BENCH: Well then, does the defense rest?

D: Am I supposed to? I don't even have a chair.

BENCH: Is there anything you want to say before I render verdict?

D: You see, sir, Hitler did terrible things and people ask, How come nobody stopped him. And we believe that

something just as terrible is going on, and we have to do something to stop it. Someone more articulate than me will explain it. I'm not very good at expressing myself.
BENCH: Verdict of this court, acquittal. Next case.

Next morning, the system relaxed. The demonstration was gone, processed four times as fast as the underclass and with no recorded incident of brutality. The average time from arrest to arraignment was a mere eight and a half hours.

2

The movement of cases has been unseasonably slow for too long, even though the crime rate is rising.

It started when the Pope came to town, and every cop had to go out on parade, making sure the Pontiff wasn't assassinated in New York City.

With no time for the bread-and-butter collars, AT-1 was deserted. Nothing came in but the bewildered junkies and hustlers of West 119th Street. That block was chosen for His Holiness to give a poor people's Mass, so there were regular police sweeps in preparation. Poor slobs didn't know what hit them.

No sooner had the Pope departed than Fidel Castro arrived. Bombs went off near the Cuban embassy, and the cops went back out in force, stretching the court holiday for another week.

It was a great time to work AT-1, but it rained throughout the Pope's tour, and turned bitter cold for Castro, and the poor police couldn't even hide in their warm cars. And nobody cared. Except for Little Joe, who handed out hot coffee, bought with his social security check, to cops on parade.

When the weather cleared, the cops went out and

brought back that one exciting day of protest, but nothing since. They'd been off their beats long enough to lose touch with their regular collars. While they were finding them, real boredom set in. AT-1 was so slow that Officer Lockheed and I were able to chant "no nukes" in unison right underneath the judge. It woke up the whole room.

3

When I was a child, policemen were seen as romantic brutes, too interested in heroics to make it in business and too lazy to learn a trade. It was a good job for a wild kid trying to settle down, or a sucker for a uniform, but low status. Crime was not a social problem then, and policemen were not well paid.

When I was an adolescent, the cops chased adolescents through the streets with tear gas and clubs. Crime had come to America, along with war and moral politics. The police became a symbol of order for some, repression for the rest, and, for the government, sandbags against the flood.

As sandbags and symbols, cops started earning a lot more money. Politicians started calling them the finest, and bumper stickers sang their praise. "Your local police," as they were called, identified no longer with the community but with the government, whose foreign war they fought right on our cities' streets.

The passion of those views is gone, overtaken by disillusionment. The public doesn't care anymore, they're just tired of living in fear. The jails are full, but the street war continues. And all reputations made in government are shot.

The police still have their exotic technology, their salaries, their camaraderie, and even their praise, but lifted up out of the community, they are more estranged than ever. Even juries don't believe them anymore. And the Police Department doesn't care, either. In their own families, cops are strangers. In their own hearts, they can't preserve the valiant-knight-in-armor stereotype.

Modern policemen, like Roman centurions, live, work, and socialize apart. They are isolated, misunderstood people—which they never intended to become. Their professional attitude makes them slam doors, stomp around, shout, shoot, and fight, but it is not personal, just something they learned how to do without ever calculating what it was doing to them. So they age quickly and deform.

It's little things, like what I did to Wazlowski at the demonstration, and what he did to me.

4

"It's different for you, homeboy," Charles said. "You don't even know what the cops do when they get uptown, and we got to live with it. Like they busted my best friend, because his girlfriend got mad at him and told the cops he had a gun. It wasn't nothing. She's the biggest liar in the projects, but they went over and broke his door down. Busted up all the furniture and pushed his mother around, and all they found was his baby brother's toy gun.

"They charged him with possession of a weapon, disorderly conduct, and some other stuff, but what would you do if they pushed your mother around?

"And they don't show no search warrants like you see on TV. Maybe for Carlo Gambino, or somebody that big, they bring a warrant, but when it's just a little minority body up in Harlem, they just take the door off and go on in. Then you got to spend the rest of the night with no damn door. In Harlem, that makes it kind of hard to fall asleep.

"See, we grew up with cops. Got chased when we were

children. See 'em come into your hooky party and make
the girls undress just to see what the boys would do. Stuff
like that. It's a different perspective."

Even Kitty was chased by the cops as a youngster, and is
where she is today because she turned down the right dark
alley and they turned down the wrong one. "The first thing
you learn is never run from a fat cop," she said. "A skinny
cop will chase you all day long. Never give up. That's the
thing about cops, they never give up. But fat cops can't
run. They shoot you."

"Yeah," said Charles. "And when it's bad uptown, it's
war. Remember the Harlem mosque? That was a war.

"This lady told a cop she was ripped off by a guy who
ran into the mosque, so they went there. Muslims told the
cops they were welcome, but, you know, this is a house of
worship. No guns allowed. The cops just laughed and went
in.

"Well, they never come out. The whole place was surrounded. They even had a helicopter shooting at it from
the air. Niggers were jumping every which way to dodge
the bullets, but I bet you didn't hear about that."

"No, but . . ."

"Them damn community relations," he said.

"My point about the cops," I said, "is what they go
through. I know what it makes them into."

"Oh, sure," said Vaughan. "Getting out the Cadillac
with stripes on their arms—these ain't no patrolmen going
into the numbers shop to pick up their money so they can
send their kids to a private school in Switzerland or someplace."

"Where do you see that?" I asked.

"Seen it when I was a hungry kid hanging out in front of
the shop. Seen it all my life."

"We all did," said Kitty. "And besides, ain't we all got
degrees in criminal justice? What do you know about it?"

5

Down at AT-1, where there are cops and personal relationships with them all over the place, opinions are scarce.

All Officer Lockheed had to say was, "You better watch yourself. You're taking this stuff too deep. Don't even bother with it, otherwise you're going to wind up in a bird cage, swinging on a little trapeze, going cheep, cheep cheep."

Al Taylor didn't want to discuss it, either. "I've been through that already. I used to hang out with these guys— go drinking with them, try to get to know them, understand. You know, the brotherhood of man. Make myself a better human being. I even ate health foods. Believe me, the whole thing was a waste of time. But I'll tell you one thing: If you meet them in court, behind the prosecutor's table, with a necktie on, it just isn't the same."

There was only Little Joe, it seemed. "No, there aren't many Jewish cops anymore, I'm sorry to say. Maybe a hundred in the whole city. There used to be thousands, and corrections officers, too. There was a time when all the captains and wardens in the Department of Corrections were Jewish."

"Really?" I asked, slightly shocked. "I didn't think Jews went in for that kind of thing."

"Well, those were good jobs," he said, "and Jews were poor."

"Yeah, but Joe, Jewish history suggests ... well, you know. Isaac Bashevis Singer once defined Yiddish as the language that was never spoken by policemen."

"Oh, I just saw something like that," Joe said, and pulled a crumpled civil service weekly out of his shopping bag. He pointed out a tiny notice: "Nobel Laureate Isaac Bashevis Singer was named Man of the Year by the Shomrim

Society, the fraternal order for Jewish members of the New York City Police Department, at its annual spiritual breakfast."

6

Officer Lockheed passed out cigars when his wife gave birth to twin girls. He hasn't had much sleep since. Looking worn, he plays the proud father.

"Goodbye, Clarence," said Joe.

"Hey, man. Why you call me Clarence? Can't you call me Lock, like everybody else?"

"I'm sorry, I thought your name was Clarence."

"Well, it is, but I'm supposed to be part American Indian, and how does it look for a one-sixteenth Cherokee blood to be called Clarence?"

"All right," said Joe, and left.

When he was gone, Officer Lockheed glared and said, "And you know they don't want no dictionaries on the Rock. They want *Hustler* magazines and *Screw* newspapers."

Lockheed is suffering and must be forgiven.

"I was the one who got up to feed the twins last night. I fed one, put it back to bed, fed the other. By then, the first one woke up, and by the time I got it to stop crying, the other one was screaming. Back and forth. I was up all night. And do you know what that woman did when I finally got back to sleep? She threw lighted matches in the bed. I'm not kidding. I woke up and the sheets were on fire. She tried to burn me up.

"So what am I supposed to do now?"

7

Kitty has announced that she is pregnant. Nothing is showing yet, but her state has softened her, even drugged her with its dreams. Fifteen generations of lost time for black people in America are going to be paid back to this baby. Ballet classes, flute lessons, maybe even organ. Some church influence, but not too much. Encyclopedias, jewelry, fine clothes, ice cream and cake. Every advantage Kitty never had is scheduled.

I thought it was an awful lot of responsibility for an unborn fetus to be carrying, which made Vaughan laugh. "Kitty's got a crummy little job, checking off boxes, the same as you. She's just trying to make that more solid in her own head, because she's got a baby coming. It ain't gonna be the easy life."

Vaughan's girlfriend is also pregnant, and he is elated. "Children are the most wonderful thing about life," he said. "It's just natural, I guess; if you love yourself, you reproduce. My children are my whole life. I hope to have as many as I can."

8

Among the ancient tribes that preceded our European tradition, the torture function consumed the entire judicial ceremony. On accusation from the king, a painful death was administered on the spot, with maximum graphic visibility. This reminded the tribe of the fury of their chief at the breaking of his peace, and it calmed them, too, as they empathized and identified their own outrage with the example provided. The effect was cathartic.

As the tribe was submerged into a larger kind of kingdom, court was held without the presence of the king. Royal power diffused from a thing demonstrated to an attitude of mind, something God and history mandated, not the king himself.

And with this new form of social organization came a new obedience. The awe of thunderbolts was replaced by an order of contract and reason. Events had to be argued, examined, and explained to display justice where once the king had stood. The truth of reason gave rise to the investigation, and with it, the torture function moved indoors. The cheapest, most efficient, and only certain outcome of an investigation is confession. So, as persuasion, and when witnesses gave conflicting testimony, or defendants refused to exercise their rights, peine forte et dure was applied to expose the truth and regulate procedure. For the survivors, uniform, humane execution followed trial.

But somewhere along this line of growth, visibility became a problem, and the metaphors began to backfire. Altercations at the gallows got out of hand and turned political. And lawyers were completing their rise.

In 1641, Parliament abolished the Star Chamber, and shortly after the Stuarts were expulsed. That was the end of the inquisition, and the beginning of court as we know it—the impartial referee, ruled by law.

The impartial court banished torture from its view, but it lingered on in obsolescence and secrecy. Finally, through modern technology, the courts learned that confession is a true bond between the accused and authority. It is not to be beaten in from outside but unburdened from within. That way, confession is the intimacy of the power relationship. From it comes penance, repentance, cleansing, and the corrective that strengthens the authoritarian bond.

In New York County, all confessions are videotaped. Suspects are more forthcoming on camera, they find. And taping it proves that no torture was used.

But once finally abolished, the torture function reappeared spontaneously, right where it started, at the tribal level of face-to-face community. Not in the mediated network of the mass society mainstream, but in the opaque pockets of poverty and abandonment, where society and life have failed most, and where the only order kept is that of the tribal king.

Law and order demand that the cop on the corner become that king. The strategies for maintaining the mainstream demand law and order. But the police have lost face, and the courts won't back them up.

At the same time that America and government were lionizing the cops, showering them with praise, wages, new toys, and huge funerals, the lawyers were moving in their own direction.

Mapp v. Ohio, 1961; *Gideon v. Wainright,* 1963; *Malloy v. Hogan,* 1963; *Escobedo v. Illinois,* 1964; the celebrated *Miranda v. Arizona,* 1966; five dozen more landmark Supreme Court decisions over the decade, and criminal procedures were thoroughly reformed. The sticky matters of search and seizure, unlawful detention, cruel and unusual punishment, self-incrimination, genuinely voluntary confession, right to counsel, and free speech were all scrutinized, redefined, and related. It took an expert to understand them, and every defendant was entitled to one.

In fact, the Bill of Rights and the Fourteenth Amendment were being forced on the criminal justice system. Not a drastic change of mind, but a series of logical clarifications and extensions of previous interpretations. Still, the legal impact was profound. The effect on the police, however, was devastating.

On apprehension, the police now had to inform their collar of all these Supreme Court decisions. Otherwise, any evidence obtained by subsequent interrogation was inadmissible in court. And, if the accused asked for the lawyer he was told he had the right to ask for, all police questioning had to cease until that lawyer arrived. In drug cases, the classic police testimony, "He threw it on the ground in front of me," would no longer suffice. Government was telling its police that they were not trusted, and not to be trusted, while the lawyers, who risked no life or limb, were.

And as these changes were being enacted, the largest investigation of police corruption ever undertaken began in New York City.

Just as police officers were coming into the pride, prosperity, and politics of increased social status, police science was made illegal.

In other, smaller jurisdictions, the Supreme Court can be overlooked, but New York is so big and so bureaucratized that it must proceed by the rules. And New York has so many isolated, immobilized, tribal poor that only torture keeps them separate from the lives and property of the mainstream.

So the job of the police has come down to standing in the ghetto and absorbing the alienation and hostility before it gets to the better neighborhoods. And keeping quiet about whatever it is that they do to survive this task.

The system's solution to the breakdown of community standards is to wear out its cops faster, throw them away, and get new ones. Most cops get tired of fighting, but only those without mortgages can quit. Some get into the torture function and make their professional performance what they really are. Some get into parking on side streets and sleeping in their car. But however they survive, they get blamed for it.

9

Although the torture function has always existed, and so has disobedience, the police go back less than 150 years. In ancient Athens the polis employed 1,200 Scythian archers to police the assembly and the law courts. The cohortes vigilum, the famous firemen of ancient Rome, also policed. And there have always been armies. But as a standing presence on the street, police emerged with the metropolitan mob, of which they are a part.

In Europe, powerful landowners traditionally feared a

standing army as a threat to their power and opposed
keeping any form of it on the streets. Thus, as the metropolis grew and introduced new forms of alienation, anonym-
ity, madness, and savagery, the power of property owners
also grew and allowed them to keep the terrifying crime-
ridden streets free of police.

But in the two centuries before this one, the European
mob sacked its capital cities at a rate of approximately
once every other generation. They became a greater threat
to property than the king. At this point, the police were
invented and, with each subsequent sacking, increased in
number. When the mob stopped revolting, the institution
stabilized.

This history of a king's army seeking public approval
created a tradition of public relations that remains among
European metropolitan police. They help the aged across
the road, give directions, and try never to do anything too
wicked or dirty while in public view.

In America, the mob was composed of immigrants of all
races and nationalities constantly fighting among themselves. Property owners had nothing to fear from them.
The American metropolis developed without police.
But the American mob feared itself. Everyone in it felt
surrounded by foreigners and sought protection from ethnic toughs. Street gangs formed and grew from protective
to aggressive, acting as government in the absence of any
other.

As the young toughs aged, their gangs became the political clubs on which legitimate metropolitan government rested. They were financed by vice and rackets,
and policed by the next generation's street gangs, who
dispatched rough justice to anyone who tried to compete
with them.

When the blue uniform was added, subsequent immigrant groups were cut out of the pie and the American po-

lice force was born. Not corrupted by professional crime, but created by it.

Gambling, prostitution, drugs (formerly liquor), and the rest of the forbidden trades have always existed within the American police system. This history has left American cops with the traditional image of tough guys with good connections who don't need to care about the public. No one asks them directions. They are volatile. They carry guns.

The first modern police force was started in London, England, in 1829. At that time, violent crime was wanton and brazen; blackmail and shakedown were commonplace. By official estimates one out of every twenty-two of the population was a career criminal. And still, public outcries of "tyrannical methods" and "despotism" greeted the arrival of professional street cops.

The first American force was the New York Police Department, begun in 1844. Its first big task was serving as "slave catchers" under the Fugitive Slave Act of 1850. From the beginning, police chiefs blamed crime on lenient judges. In 1857, a state investigation of police corruption led to the creation of a separate state police force, which was repelled by a larger force when it stormed city police headquarters. And so on. It took a long time to clean up the image.

People have never called the cops unless they feared something worse. Police behavior has always been tolerated because it falls upon the powerless.

10

In books and on television, cops spend their time fighting an evil that is usually tinged with genius and glamour. In real life, they spend the day with the failed and the broken and the crazy, dealing with the aberrations of human behavior that no one else can bear. They are the political janitors of the very bottom of the social pyramid. Civilization has no meaning for them, but their job is to save it.

My heart goes out to police officers. They lie on wet pavement for eleven hours in midwinter on a routine stakeout. They swing off roofs on ropes to save a suicide, and go back to the same corner their partner was murdered at, a week later. Cops are brave and self-sacrificing. They are the last strangers who rush indiscriminately to the aid of those imperiled, and I am as grateful and admiring as anyone.

But how can they work for the status quo, given what they know about it? And how does bravery look when just a radio call away is the full might of authority's reinforcements, all the way up to the hydrogen bomb.

My heart goes out to police officers, but doesn't it occur to them that their heroics go unsung because their kind of masculine madness and sacrifice hurts people and provokes them? Can't they see that their duty and suffering are also making the situation worse? The holy war they fight to keep their suburban families from ever having to know about has already reached the suburbs. They are part of a crumbling order, and they are not preventing decay by the way they treat people.

As if it were their fault, for they are crumbling, too.

Force is physical power. To yield to it is an act of necessity, not will. Force creates no sense of moral duty in the enforced. Morality comes from caring about others, from identifying other lives with your own. But the police cannot address social problems except by enforcement, and in this society, that means force.

In a typical year in New York, seven police officers die in the line of duty, twenty-nine are wounded, and eight more commit suicide. In that same time, seven black or

Hispanic youths are killed by white policemen under questionable circumstances.

11

Most cops, even when you meet them behind the prosecutor's table, seem ordinary, shopping-mall-educated carriers of conventional reactionary ideals. But exceptions abound.

Officer Fly plays backgammon on the clerk's desk with casino flair. Officer Salt wears a jacket monogrammed for his yacht, *The AT-1*, because that's where he earned the money to pay for it. Officer Coke looks like a football player: he has no neck, a shaved head, and a one-syllable style. But under his bulging bicep is a thick volume entitled *Nuclear Physics*. Coke went to a special school for gifted children and has always liked to keep up on the sciences. Officer Culley, immortalized on the shithouse walls, looks like a TV newscaster. Officer Louie "Snake" Belleview comes to court in shorts and no shirt, showing off his tattoo-covered body—mostly snakes. Officer Loam takes gruesome snapshots of dead junkies and keeps them in an album called *Harlem Views*, which he painstakingly lettered on the cover.

In the third row of the audience, a suave cop sits with his arms around his prisoner's wife, trying to make some time. She smiles back through the tears, trying to help her husband. At the bridge, a huge, drunken cop passes out cold on the night-court floor, too fat to be dragged away without interrupting the proceedings. Over on the prisoner's bench, a distraught police officer tenderly comforts a twelve-year-old prostitute runaway, assuring her that she can stay with his estranged wife on Staten Island.

There are gay cops who wear rouge, and cops who collect antiques. There are poets on the police force, and Muslim detectives. A young cop with a goatee just graduated from art school, and a magnificent white-haired old lady who speaks three languages is a crack senior detective for the pickpocket and confidence squad. The stereotype has thirty thousand different faces, each mask contradicting the impression that came before.

People who come to court generally bring something to read. Cops mostly carry *Reader's Digest* condensed novels and shiny paperback thrillers with one-word titles. But AT-1 has also seen: *The Memoirs of Field Marshal Kietel, 1938 to 1945; The Complete Book of Patio Gardening; Summerhill; Accidental Networks: A History of Witchcraft; The Vikings in Britain; Finnegans Wake; Mein Kampf;* and various works by Winston Churchill, Wilhelm Reich, Thomas Hardy, Theodore Dreiser, and Dostoevsky.

In summer, cops come to court in T-shirts that say: *I'm so happy I could just shit; Ass, gas, and grass; Ninth Precinct—Jungle Habitat; Misfit; Always be safe, sleep with a cop; Midnight Task Force; Keep on suckin'; Intercourse, Pennsylvania; Goyim for Jesus;* and *Eat Here,* with an index pointing downward.

Acne and eczema, gum-chewing, and general jumpiness are also indicators of tension, but lately I just keep track of the eyes. Most cops aren't crazy. It's only the few with the dilated pupils who will still go one-on-one down a dark alley and watch what they risked their life to catch walk out of court paroled. Or who bring in a messed-up kid because they think he needs help, and plead with the court for compassion, and care about the kid whom the flow shoves into the bureaucratic jungle. The glint in the eyes says that they are crazy enough to kill or still in the running for sainthood, but not which.

12

BRIDGEMAN: Docket Number Y930843, Jeffrey Cow, charged with 195.05, obstructing governmental operations, and 205.30, resisting arrest, on the complaint of Officer Pickle.

PA: Your honor, my client is a former schoolteacher in this city and is now the conductor of an orchestra in Philadelphia. This is a nothing case, will you dismiss it?

BENCH: If the people will consent.

A/O: Look, I'm willing to give this guy a break, but I don't want to get sued. Can't you make him plead to something, so at least I can protect myself?

DA: Well, what happened, exactly, Officer?

A/O: I was making this collar for aggravated assault. The guy was a real psycho. He was beating me with this steel cane. Just as I was cuffing him, this guy turns up and completely misunderstands everything. He starts shouting at me to let him go, he's crippled. You can't beat a cripple. He carries on like this for approximately two minutes. By this time, a crowd gathered, and with an audience, the psycho went berserk. So I collared both of them. How did I know he was in the orchestra?

DA: I can't dismiss the case . . .

BRIDGEMAN: Docket Number Y938464, Divine Justice, charged with petit larceny and assault on the complaint of Officer Threadgill.

BENCH: Before we start, could you all change sides, please?

A/O: No. This is right. I've been on the force sixteen years. Over twenty-two hundred arrests, and every time I come to court, I always stand on this side.

BENCH: But we're undergoing renovations, and temporarily it's set up the other way around.

A/O: You see, your honor, most cops are right-handed. The gun is on the right side. If we switch places, a defendant could reach over and—

BENCH: Officer!

A/O: All right. You make the law, what do I know? I'm just a cop.

DA: Tell me, Officer, did he do it?

A/O: Counselor, why do you think I arrested him?

DA: Okay, okay. Tell me about it.

A/O: They're friends. They first met in jail. And they're, uh, kind of close. It was a lovers' quarrel. He beat him up and took some clothes.

DA: Well, what do you want me to do with it?

A/O: I don't give a damn. You can scribble the whole thing out if you want. You're the one that's paid to think. I'm just the cop. I'm not allowed to think. If someone complains, I'm ordered to make the arrest. I'm of very limited intelligence, can't you tell?

DA: But if you don't care, why did you make the arrest?

A/O: Because I thought someone might get hurt or killed, and I didn't want to take the chance.

DA: Your honor, may we approach?

A/O: Twenty-two hundred times I've been in court and I never stood on this side before. Oops, I did once . . . in alimony court.

LAS: No need to approach, there will be no plea. My client insists it was a fair fight.

D: All the time he hassles me, what I'm supposed to do?

BENCH: Paroled, two weeks please.

BRIDGEMAN: Ten/fifteen.

BENCH: October 15, paroled.

BENCH: What's this man's problem, Officer?

A/O: He should have listened when Jimmy Cagney said, "Never steal anything small," in 1959.

BENCH: I'm afraid I fail . . .

A/O: Or was it *Angels with Dirty Faces,* 1938.

BENCH: Never mind.

A/O: This guy must go out every night. I catch him about once a week.

BENCH: How?

A/O: This one was easy. He went in, and the door locked

behind him, so he couldn't get out. We got a call from the burglar alarm.

BENCH: What is the premises?

A/O: The old Sperry Rand building. Now it's the Institute of Aeronautics and Astronautics.

BENCH: I see, some sort of architectural group.

A/O: No. Aeronautics is flying within the atmosphere. And astro means beyond—flying beyond the atmosphere. In space.

BRIDGEMAN: Docket Number Y942479, Charles Cheeks, charged with the possession of marijuana as a violation.

DA: Officer, this is the worst case I've seen all week.

A/O: I know what you mean. He's a totally obnoxious little fucker. As a matter of fact, he reminds me of my wife.

DA: That's not what I meant. This case is so bad I don't know how it ever got written up. It should never have got this far.

A/O: Well, you know, when you can't afford to go away, you gotta stay home and collar up.

WRITE-UP: A/O observes beat drug sale. D flees and is captured. One lead pipe, one straight razor, fifteen marijuana cigarettes. The above is a complete list of all items vouchered.

LAS: I am not maintaining that my client lives in the Hilton Hotel, but in a Hilton Hotel. The spelling is probably different.

A/O: Is he kidding? I know the guy. He sleeps in the street.

LAS: And besides, the search is questionable.

A/O: Where is he getting his information, out of his asshole?

DA: No, from the defendant. That's how this system works.

A/O: Oh, no wonder . . .

DA: Your honor, this was an obvious sale. The search is good.

LAS: Drugs! My client is charged with fraudulent accosting and a weapon. There's no mention of drugs in the complaint.

A/O: Fifteen marijuana cigarettes were vouchered!

LAS: And you're offering a plea to disorderly conduct?

A/O: Disorderly conduct? For this scum bag? I know him from the park. He soaks cigars in vodka, crumbles them up, rolls them into joints, and sells them. The pipe and the razor are for dissatisfied customers. He's bad, and you're letting him off with disorderly conduct?

DA: And he's refused the offer.

BENCH: I guess we'll have to adjourn this for motions. October 24 in AE-5. Paroled, on the consent of the People.

A/O: How could you consent to parole? This guy doesn't even have a name and an address.

DA: C'mon, Officer. There were no drugs. We've got no case.

A/O: I don't know. There's something wrong here. I guess it's me.

DA: What can I tell you. There's 100,000 cases a year to prosecute, and this one just doesn't make it.

A/O: Yeah. I know all about it. Last week I had an undercover drug sale. The law says it's a felony, but you guys reduced it to a misdemeanor possession and gave him time served. What am I knocking myself out for?

DA: Officer, the resources of this office must be concentrated on the most serious cases.

A/O: Please don't tell me about it. It doesn't take very long on this job to realize that it ain't honest. You know, I never wanted to be anything but a cop. My father and grandfather were cops, but little by little it takes over your whole life. First your spare time goes, then your hobbies. Then you even have to let your wife and family go to hang in and be a cop. You give up everything, and for what? This kind of shit.

DA: Okay, relax.

A/O: Oh, I don't want to argue. I've seen it too many times before. I know better than to get involved. I don't care if it's 90 days, time served or you give him a bowl of soup and five dollars. I'm getting to an age where right and wrong doesn't mean so much anymore. I just get mad about it sometimes.

BRIDGEMAN: Docket Number Y944960, Sulester Sessoms, charged with assault, obstruction, and a resist, on complaint of Officer Bismal.

CW: I just want to ask you a question.

A/O: You always want to ask me a question. Later; we're in court.

CW: Can they let him go? He broke my windshield and cost me two days' work, and . . .

A/O: I already told you they'll probably ask for restitution. Just tell them it cost $300 and don't say anything else.

BENCH: Step up, gentlemen.

The defendant left his car overtime at a parking meter, then punched the driver of the tow truck taking it away and broke the windshield of said truck. The bench conference is brief.

LAS: My client agrees to make retribution.

DA: No, Counselor, we make retribution. Your client makes restitution.

LAS: Restitution, of course.

BENCH: Okay, how much does a windshield cost?

CW: $300.

BENCH: $300! What is it made of, platinum?

CW: Well, I'm not really sure.

BENCH: Okay, second call to verify the price of a windshield.

CW: What does this mean?

A/O: Didn't I tell you just to say $300? We could have been out of here. Now we have to wait.

CW: Your honor, I just want to ask you this: How can they let him go just because he pays for the windshield? I mean, he hit me.

A/O: Shut up. Do you hear me? Just keep your mouth shut. I'll explain everything afterward. Just don't say nothing.

CW: But they're going to let him go.

A/O: I said shut up. Every time you open your mouth, you keep us here an extra half day. I mean, mister, this is not a homicide. I got a wife and kids. I'd like to see them . . .

BRIDGEMAN: Docket Number Y945315, Karl Lunch, charged with gambling, on the complaint of Officer Headley, and Docket Number Y945422, Karl Cleo, charged with assault, on the complaint of Officer Spam.

BENCH: C'mon. Let's go, let's go.

DA: Are you Spam?

A/O: No, I'm Headley. Spam is at home, in a neck brace. I was assigned to the misdemeanor case originally. I just want to go home now. I've been here two solid days.

BENCH: We can't arraign this, we don't have fingerprints.

A/O: What?

LAS: I have prints here.

DA: I do, too.

BENCH: I'm confused. Can you help me, Officer?

A/O: He's a gambler. I've busted him before, myself. After I picked him up and printed him, we were bringing him to court when he assaulted my partner in the radio car. Put him in the hospital.

BENCH: Why wasn't he handcuffed?

A/O: He was. He kicked him in the head.

BENCH: But you didn't print him.

A/O: What do you mean? He's been printed.

BENCH: I see. You printed him on the misdemeanor, not the felony.

A/O: What difference does it make? He was in police custody all the time in between.

BENCH: That's the law, Officer. Take him back and print him.

A/O: Oh, no, not me. I haven't slept in two days. This isn't even my arrest. I'm done.

BRIDGEMAN: Corrections can't accept him until he's been printed.

A/O: I won't.

BENCH: You must.

BRIDGEMAN: . . . James Polite, charged with 240.55, reporting a false incident in the third degree.

LAS: This is a classic St. Patrick's Day incident, your honor. My client is not a criminal. He was sitting in a coffee shop when he noticed three men in blue jeans and leather jackets leaning on his station wagon with guns drawn. He became alarmed and dialed the police emergency number. When the three men entered the coffee shop, my client saw that they were drunk and bolted. They chased him home and arrested him.

BENCH: Didn't they identify themselves as police officers?

D: They had a badge, but they were drunk. I couldn't believe . . .

BENCH: What about it, Officers?

A/O: We got a radio call to check out the station wagon.

CPS: What's the matter, Officer? You look upset.

P/O: My collar just undressed in the cells and won't put his clothes back on.

CPS: Gee, that's too bad.

P/O: Last week I picked up a drunk wandering around in the middle of 125th Street. When I got him in the car, I found out he had nothing on underneath his coat.

CPS: Terrible.

P/O: Tuesday I got a collar, and after the strip search, he wouldn't get dressed. And now this. Three straight times, I have to come to court with a naked body. I'm going nuts. Do you know the odds against it happening?

CPS: No idea.

P/O: It's way over 13 million to 1, I can tell you that.

VOUCHER NUMBER Q879142. Quantity: one. Description: English sheep dog, white. Value: $250.

WRITE-UP: D runs up to nine-year-old child, pushes child, and grabs leashed dog. D and friend them jump into taxi and leave. Child lives next door to D and is the daughter of a police officer. When he got home, he made the arrest and vouchered the dog as evidence.

A/O: Counselor, this has nothing to do with the dog. This has to do with pushing a nine-year-old child and taking property from her. This is a crime.

DA: What do you expect me to do?

A/O: I don't know. My daughter just wants her dog back. I don't know what's going on. We bought her this dog three years ago, and all of a sudden this bitch shows up from next door and says it's her dog. She's got a photograph or something.

PA: There is no crime here, your honor. The dog belongs to my client. I know this dog myself, personally. This is ridiculous.

BENCH: Save your wind, sir. This matter must be litigated.

P/O: I didn't know you played football, you should try and get into our league.

UCO: Can I?

P/O: Well, at the beginning of the season, it was limited to the precincts, but by now half the league is out with injuries. They let just about anybody in.

UCO: Great.

P/O: We got one rule, though. If you hurt somebody, it's your responsibility to take them down to the police surgeon and sign them in.

LAS: Who's the prearraignment officer tonight?
BRIDGEMAN: Larry.
LAS: Larry? Is he the big guy with all the hair and the beard?
BRIDGEMAN: You know who Larry is, the freak.
P/O: I am not a freak.
BRIDGEMAN: Aw c'mon, man, everybody knows all you do is get high and boogie. You're probably high right now.
P/O: You think I'm high every night, and you know damn well I can't afford to get high every night. I've got a mortgage. But next Friday, I sure will be. It's my birthday, and my wife is taking me to see the Grateful Dead.
BRIDGEMAN: You're not going to see that bunch of freaks?
P/O: They are not freaks. They used to be, but not anymore. Have you listened to their last album?

A/O: The offer is what?
DA: I said, a plea to petit larceny and a conditional discharge. Can you live with that, Officer?
A/O: I can live with it, but there are over two thousand hours of overtime in this case.
DA: On one box of salami?
A/O: There were three hundred pounds of salami in that box.
DA: So?
A/O: Look, son. It took two years to find this guy and catch him with the meat in his forklift. Who knows how much he got away with before that.
DA: I'm afraid everything but the box of salami is allegation.
A/O: Hey, what are you, some kind of vegetarian or something?

The old cop looked up from his book and turned to the young cop. "You're a police officer. You might get a kick out of this," he said. The young cop nodded, and the old cop began to read aloud:

> Lady Macleod, confident and sure of herself, tried to crack Dr. Johnson's cynicism by asking whether human beings were not possessed of natural goodness.
> JOHNSON: No, madam, no more than wolves.
> LADY MACLEOD: This is worse than Swift!

The old cop chuckled.

"Say, who is this Dr. Johnson?" asked the young cop.

"He's the man who wrote the dictionary," said the old cop.

"Then I want to know about him," said the young cop, copying down the author and title from the cover of the book. "You never can tell, there might be a question about it on the next promotional test."

CHAPTER SIX

1

One morning, after punching in, Vaughan and I went out for a walk and breakfast, to kill time before court began. Vaughan held a tabloid in his armpit, and I had a big paper, folded up, under mine. Along the way, we stopped at a kiosk and each bought a pack of cigarettes.

"How about the paper?" the vendor asked Vaughan.

"What about it?" Vaughan answered.

"You buying that paper, mister?"

"I already bought it, in Brooklyn, early this morning. See, it's a Brooklyn edition."

"Oh," said the vendor, and handed down the cigarettes.

We moved on. I didn't think anything of it, but Vaughan was furious. "He didn't ask you where you got your paper, did he? Do you think he would ask me if I was white? Why are they always asking black people if they're stealing something?"

"Well, you don't know where he's coming from," I started to say.

"I know," he cut me off, "I'm being oversensitive. Maybe his boss just yelled at him because he lost some papers. Or anything. It could have nothing to do with this black-white thing out here—but why are there all these little reminders, all day long, that I am black? I got nothing against white people. I teach my kids not to hate white people. I'd just as soon forget the whole thing. But they make it so I have to deal with it all the time, even when it's not there.

"It ain't the paper. I consider that just ordinary dealing with life," he said. "Yesterday, I got called nigger. I was coming back from my aunt's house, and it was so nice I decided to walk. I cut through Bensonhurst. That's where I went to primary school. All white and middle-class. They bussed us in.

"I was remembering how integrated I was, going in their houses and everything. Big houses. And thinking how good it would be to live there now, with the trees and a big lawn. I saw this little white kid walking up to me, and I was thinking he must be about the same age as my son, when he called me a nigger."

"What did you do?"

"What could I do. I couldn't hit a little kid."

"I don't know."

"But it reminded me. Made me realize what the deal is, and what the deal was never meant to be. You know how they say orphans spend their lives searching for their parents. That's how black people are, searching for their home. I can never be at home in America. I'm black. I want to go to Africa. I've never been there. I don't know what it is. I'm quite sure it's no better than any other social democratic system, but at least I'll be home. I don't belong here, and they never let me forget it.

"Damn," he said, tossing his paper into a pile of garbage swirling on the street.

We went on to breakfast, but Vaughan wasn't hungry. "When slavery ended, it was our time to come North and get those new jobs in industry. But there was famine in Ireland, so America took their hungry and gave them work. And then they took every other kind of white people who would work cheap. We had to wait an extra hundred years just to come up here. And now that it's our time, all the jobs are going down South, where we came from.

"What they called desegregation was—they closed the black-run schools, and they built roads and gave mortgages to white people, so they could go to the suburbs and leave us behind in segregated, white-controlled schools. What they called integration was stealing our culture. And I'm supposed to believe it wasn't planned that way?

"You notice how when black people get welfare, it demeans them. They all stigmatized and lose their self-esteem. But when America can't sell wheat to the Russians, the government gives the grain dealers $30 million, and nobody feels demeaned or stigmatized, or nothing. If black people owned that wheat, there would be a million reasons for why the program failed.

"It was all designed to fail. Black people living in America was just not meant to be."

2

In the suburbs around New York, burning crosses turn up, sporadically, on the lawns of black families, and a black computer executive had his house bombed in Yonkers. The newspapers are certain that this is not the work of any organized body, such as the Ku Klux Klan, but merely juvenile pranks. When they burned crosses in rural Mississippi twenty years ago, New York considered it medieval barbarity. Now, it's a prank.

An assistant police chief, being interviewed in the afternoon paper, said, as if it were science, "Forty percent of all ten-year-olds in Harlem carry guns and will commit seven to nine felonies before they are old enough to be prosecuted for them."

The most unbelievable news comes from the jungles of South America, where a religious colony of predominantly black North Americans followed their leader and drank a fruit cordial of Kool-Aid and cyanide; 911 died. It was the largest mass suicide in known history, and the first to take place without imminent threat.

They left a tape recorder rolling, so the world could hear the last sermon and their convulsions, and know they died in spite, certain that America would recoil in guilt when it realized what it had done to these poor, good, Christian people.

America never even knew the gesture was being made, and didn't care to. We accept that history is indifferent to self-regarding gestures. We are learning that the fact that we exist does not inspire a sense of obligation on the part of the universe.

3

America was such a good idea, and slavery such a bad one. Our Founding Fathers were "calm good men who strived toward righteousness. Not wicked," but soft on slavery. And that moral oversight, a tiny flicker of nightmare in the nation they envisioned, has grown to become the significant core of the American experience.

We fought a Civil War over it, and rearranged our Constitution to obliterate every conceivable trace. But the friction lingers, now coded as equal opportunity, free abortion, the death penalty, and welfare. The pain between the races helped create our unique American forms of art, speech, and athletics, as well as our worst national crimes and guilts. But for all the attention, obsession, resources, and history, whether it waxes or wanes, blows violent or calm, this black-white thing will not improve.

So, for whom does AT-1 represent justice?

Defendants tend to believe they are innocent, even though they rarely are, because the procedures they encounter on arrest evoke a historical rather than a judicial sense. A sense of oppression rather than of guilt—"There ain't no telling what the white man might do." He's cool, inscrutable, crazy, and cruel, the same as he's always been.

Every morning, when the jail buses arrive, they unload their prisoners into a courtyard behind the pens. A metal door rolls down and locks the courtyard before the bus door opens. The prisoners march out of the bus in a column of twos. Silent, downcast, arms out, feet in step. They are handcuffed in pairs. Running down the line through every pair of handcuffs is a long heavy chain. The chain swings, and all the prisoners are black.

Not all crimes are political, but all punishments are. And we come from such a shoddy tradition.

4

People have been enslaved since time began. Most slaveries tied people to land as much as to masters, and gave them certain legal and religious rights, just because they were human. American slaves all had prices, but no rights, no space, and no time. For many, the material conditions were no worse than those of the free factory workers of the time, but they were property, pure and simple. Assault and battery of a slave was not a criminal offense. A slave's testimony was not admissible in court. Slaves held no assets, had no legal families, and couldn't even keep their children.

This "peculiar institution" produced two separate societies in the same place. Everyone had a second personality for dealing with the other race. Ignorance between the races was preserved, while intimacy was allowed. It was one of the craziest and most difficult social forms ever to flourish.

Masters can love their slaves, but cannot trust them, because slaves always want to escape. Slaves can love their masters, but they can never forgive them. For masters and for slaves, the intimacy is never as real as the fear.

But in America, slave women raised the master's children, and the white mistress usually took charge of rearing the slave children. The black and white children played together, but at the age of puberty, they were expected to revert. Then came sex, which in those days was a forbidden sinful act and therefore easily stimulated by racism, and proprietary rights. And religion, which the Christians forced on the Africans, and then feared when they embraced it.

Slave owners were determined to get their crops to market, and their souls to heaven, and couldn't be honest. Slaves had no guns, no army, and no navy. Their only political tools were cunning and deceit. Their only space, ambiguity.

Of what the master saw as fine cuisine, the slave who cooked it said, "How many times I spit in the biscuits and peed in the coffee to get back at them."

Or what the master saw as a nigger stealing his chickens, the slave saw as a mere accounting entry. Debit chickens, and credit for fed slaves receivable. Since both belonged to the master, nothing had changed hands. Besides, they reasoned, if buckra was not a thief, what were they doing here?

Masters named their slaves, often humorously, and those

were their legal names. Surnames were forbidden. To the slaves, these names were just part of the job. Among themselves, they had real names and surnames, identifying with the land they belonged to. As in feudal Scotland or Japan, not the land they occupied, but their grandmother's, or as far back as they could trace.

When slavery ended, the slaves departed immediately, leaving their slave names and brokenhearted masters behind. There was some nostalgia, but it was not widespread.

The Civil War crushed Southern power. Cotton ruined its soil. Emancipation began with a rash of lawsuits brought by former slaves against racial discrimination and thrown out of court by former Confederate judges. Soon the plantation was reorganized into sharecropping on the feudal model, shaping the new freedom into what it had been before.

Slaves were born to life sentences of hard labor and couldn't be punished much further for crime. With freedom came the penitentiary, the chain gang, and the practice of convict leasing. These highly competitive labor sources soon drove the demand for prisoners far beyond the natural supply of rising crime and into open persecution.

After slavery came the rise of the Klan, mobbings, lynchings, Black Codes forbidding everything down to non-agricultural labor, apartheid laws, and so on. Then began white resentment, white fear, and the loss of protection afforded to property with a high cash value.

What the owners of slaves had lost in war, the owners of machines had won. But the winners had already figured out that labor is easier to manage if you don't feed, clothe, and house it. Autonomous, independent individuals feel more responsible for themselves, despair more easily, and consequently are more likely to do as they are told. The winners didn't want the slaves.

It took a century for black America to be driven off
the land and move North to the cities. During this time,
the standard and quality of life were raised for everyone,
but blacks remained, as ever, without material means in a
materialist society. Racism endures, and so does its politics.

5

"I'm sorry," said Little Joe. "All this is wrong. Didn't I tell
you to read the *Autobiography of Lincoln Steffens*?"

"I guess you did."

"Well, read it. Read the beginning, when he was a
young police reporter covering this system. It was the
same as it is today, only the defendants were all Jews from
the Lower East Side. They even had a liberal reformer
named Henry Goddard, in those days, who proved by IQ
tests that 83 percent of all immigrant Jews were feeble-
minded. And then came the Italians with their criminal
proclivity. That's how it's always been for the poor.

"Believe me, you could release 90 percent of the inmates at Rikers Island right now, with no danger to the
community whatsoever, if you could find them a place to
live and a job. You know, a young man likes to have a few
dollars. He wants to have a car so he can take his mother
out for a ride, and his girlfriend. He wants to show he is a
man, and if he can't get a job or keep an apartment, he
can't be a man until he commits a crime. It's been going on
for four hundred years, and if you would read up on it, you
wouldn't have to be ignorant."

"It's not to do with knowledge, Joe. AT-1 just feels like a
plantation. Ask anyone."

"You don't know what you're talking about," Joe said.
"Terrible crimes really happen all the time. Victims suffer
terrible effects. Terrible—. 'The bullet speeds, the ax falls,

the trap springs, and that's the end.' A crime, and something must be done, even though it's too late."

6

When individuals cannot relate what they give to work with what they receive, there is no workmanship and no responsibility, just passivity, neglect and the belief that everything in life comes from outside. This is despair, and the belief in miracles.

It feels like servitude. Earnings seem like an accident or a favor. This feeling provokes the fear that the power that keeps you is someplace to which you have no access. Without access, you are nothing. And when you are nothing, the loathing of the workplace pervades all the relationships that go on there. Shame arrests lamentation, and they own you.

The office of the Manhattan DA is very sensitive to racism. Part of their job interview for whites is telling you that you will be around black and Hispanic people and that no racial prejudice whatsoever will be tolerated. The office hired their first black lawyer in 1905, but there wasn't a black judge until 1932. One of the big white bosses does volunteer work with disadvantaged minority teenagers on weekends. Several of their most important lawyers are black, as is the vast majority of the support staff.

Their morality says that the racist tradition was to abandon and ignore the ghetto. The preponderance of black defendants, for them, shows enlightenment. The black community is finally getting the police protection its decent citizens have always asked for.

But our social order comes with a legacy of great exactness in contracts and the administration of property relationships, and great insensitivity in human relationships.

"Go ahead, man, you can slap my palm like a brother," says the job-secure court part specialist to some big-shot white DA. And the big shot, so high up nobody even knows what he does, cringes and declines to slap.

Among its black support staff, the office is considered absolutely racist and prejudiced. The racism is institutional, not overt. Instead of an overseer, there is a surveillance from inside the personality. The self surrendered for observation and counting. And every move made in self-conscious calculation for the invisible all-seeing authority, which acts in symbols as subtle as an underarm newspaper.

7

BENCH: Why is that woman crying?

BRIDGEMAN: You'd be crying too if you had thirty-five warrants outstanding against you.

A/O: Are you kidding, she's got seventy-six prior arrests. She knows the system better than I do. She's just an actress.

BENCH: Well, then, maybe she's crying because she knows how much trouble she's in.

A/O: Go on.

On the prisoner's bench, the awaiting defendant pulls out a newspaper and opens it. "No reading allowed," the court officers scream in unison as the defendant is struck by an epileptic fit. The whole court turns to see the morning paper fly up in the air and come apart, swirling slowly down, sheet by sheet, and spreading to cover the spasming body.

COURT REPORTER: What's the matter, is this your first fit?

BENCH: No, but . . .

A/O: Your honor, he's faking. He's only trying to delay the case. He was okay yesterday, and he was okay in the pens, five minutes ago . . .

BENCH: Well, these things can come up suddenly. Second call. Next case.

Docket Number Y953669, Al Green, charged with display-ing a .22 pistol with six live rounds and brandishing it. D is forty-nine years old, married twenty-seven years, on the same job for thirty years, a Boy Scout leader for ten years, and has no criminal record.

LAS: My client informs me, and the court through counsel, that on two previous occasions, if he didn't have a gun on him, he wouldn't be alive to be facing these charges. The junkies have taken over his building. The defendant wishes to ask how he is going to survive in this jungle without it.

BENCH: Paroled . . .

BRIDGEMAN: Docket Number Y966311, Clevester Rumph, charged with 140.15, theft of services, on the complaint of Officer Wiltshire, Transit.

Mr. Rumph is a farebeat, the least serious of all possible criminal types. He slipped into the subway without paying.

LAS: My client is fifty-nine years of age, and seems to be suffering some mental disorder, but he is neither a violent nor an unpleasant man, and given the nature of the charges, the severity of a psychiatric examination would be unwarranted. So on behalf of my client, I am going to enter a plea of guilty as charged, but I urge the court to consider that for a man in this condition to spend half the night handcuffed to a sink in a disused subway washroom is punishment enough.

D: I do not want this man.

BENCH: What do you mean, you don't want him? He's your legal representative in this court.

D: I do not belong in this court. I am a Prince of Africa, your honor. For fourteen years, I have worked for peace between nations. Therefore, I am entitled to diplomatic immunity. I cannot be held on these charges.

BENCH: Isn't that interesting.

D: Yes.

BENCH: As a matter of fact, I find that a brilliant defense. I'm dismissing this case.

DA: Over the objection of the People.

BENCH: Counselor, don't be a shmuck.

BRIDGEMAN: Return on warrant, Docket Number Z889155, Horace Clark. Warrant signed by Judge Blud, in Brooklyn.

D is wearing a woman's stocking for a hat, a foulard scarf rolled and tied into a loincloth, and nothing else.

D: I can't take any more!

BRIDGEMAN: Shut up and stand still. Let your lawyer do the talking.

D: No! I cannot stand this anymore. My wife died of disease, my daughter was killed by a prostitute, and you arrest me because I went to Ohio for my mother's funeral. This is the end. When I pull my stocking down, I renounce my American citizenship, I deny this court. And I no longer answer to the name of Horace Clark.

D pulls stocking over face and is carried out rigid.

BENCH: Did you get all that, Al?

COURT REPORTER: I got more than that.

BENCH: What is that supposed to mean?

COURT REPORTER: I didn't say anything.

BRIDGEMAN: Docket Number—

BENCH: Wait. Don't start yet. I want to have a word with the court reporter.

COURT REPORTER: Have as many as you like.

BENCH: What is it, Al? Ever since you've come back on days, you're only here half the time. And even when you're here, you're not here half the time. Are your hands cold? Do your fingers feel stiff?

COURT REPORTER: No, I don't get cold.

BENCH: I'm hip. So what is it?

COURT REPORTER: Oh, it's an ethnic problem, your honor. I got a shylock in Jersey and I have to keep going over there to pay him. I don't know why I do it. It's just a masochistic thing. At least, that's what my psychiatrist tells me, and he costs even more.

BENCH: You see what I get to work with? And they expect dispositions. But you're back from Jersey now, I take it.

COURT REPORTER: We're all waiting on you, your honor. You're the judge here, aren't you?

BENCH: Mr. Court Reporter, what are you inhaling down there?

The court reporter looks into the bag at his feet, filled with beer, wine, fruit juice, and spices.

COURT REPORTER: It's my special tonic. Three different kinds of beer in it and . . . well, it's kind of a Bloody Mary, more or less.

BENCH: Please. Can we just proceed?

COURT REPORTER: If someone will run out and get me a box of Fig Newtons—

BRIDGEMAN: Docket Number Y967128. The Right Reverend Rogers—

COURT REPORTER: Stop! I can't hear any of that . . .

A/O brings up D, obscured by his sweeping black cape with purple lining and large fuzzy purple hat. D places hat on bridge and stretches to the bench or heaven. Court is in commotion.

D: Your honor. I am the Playboy Messiah. I travel all over the world bringing the teachings of Jesus to the wild element. They too are the children of God!

BENCH: Oh, dear.

COURT REPORTER: I guess you know the Reverend Rogers by now; he's down here all the time.

BENCH: No. On what charges?

COURT REPORTER: Oh, this and that.

UCOs grab D and hold his hands to his sides.

BRIDGEMAN: No waving.

D: Hey, get your hands off me. I'm an attorney-at-law— I'm practicing here. I'm a man of the Lord, you have no right to touch me.

BRIDGEMEN: Speak through your lawyer, mister. It's for your own good.

D: I don't need that boy.

BENCH: Mr. Rogers, the Constitution guarantees you many rights. Without the services of a lawyer, those rights will not protect you. Besides, the Legal Aid Society has provided you with an excellent attorney. One of the best. You would be foolish to refuse him, in light of the advantages.

D: I am not refusing him. As a matter of fact, I was just reminding him, back there, of the time we had cocktails together, over at Peggy Doyle's.

LAS: For the record, we never had cocktails together. Not at Peggy Doyle's or anywhere else.

D: You see, your honor? But in spite of his unwillingness, I will not cast him out. But there is something I must explain.

BENCH: I warn you, you could be damaging your case.

D: I am the Playboy Messiah. I travel the earth, bringing the Lord's word to hepcats and undesirables. It's all right here in this briefcase. Pictures of me with the mayor, and the governor, and with Presidents. I have intimate friends on the City Council and in the Congress down in Washington. And I will call all of them to testify as character witnesses. Here is my proof.

D opens briefcase and turns it upside down. Papers, snapshots, and clippings wash across the ready cases on the bridge and fall on the floor.

CPS: You think he knows the mayor, even?

COURT REPORTER: Sure. You can't get but so far in this town before you run into Reverend Sugar Rogers.

Bridgeman stuffs papers back into briefcase and holds it.

BENCH: Now, ah, Reverend. What's this about refusing to pay the taxi fare?

CW: That's right, your honor—

BENCH: Hold it. Who are you? Put your name and address on the record and who you are.

CW: Ben Cohen, 25 Pleasant Street. I'm the taxi driver. He made me drive up and down Water Street because he didn't know what number he wanted. Finally, I put him out and he refused to pay. He was drunk.

DA: Look, Mr. Cohen. No spontaneous outbursts. If you've got something to say, you tell me first, okay?

BENCH: Is this true?

LAS: My client informs me that we have no plea.

BENCH: Everybody come up here. You, too, taxi driver. Why can't we just arrange restitution?

They confer.

COURT REPORTER: Reverend Rogers used to be a real fine figure. Had himself a big church up in Harlem, and was friends with Martin Luther King. He was a power in the black community. Even had himself photographed with Nelson Rockefeller and John Lindsay. I guess he met them at Louis Armstrong's funeral.

BENCH: Step back, we're just wasting time.

COURT REPORTER: Somewhere along the line, the reverend broke down. That can happen to black talent.

D: Your honor. The thirty-eighth President of the United States, Gerald R. Ford, who happens to be a friend— he rolled over in bed, grabbed his dear wife, Betty, and held her close while he wrestled with his conscience. In the morning, he pardoned Richard Nixon of all crimes. And I'm asking you, today, to exercise that same spirit here.

BENCH: It's not within my powers. I sit here only to set bail or parole, and in order to parole you I must have a reason. Frankly, Mr. Rogers, from looking at your past record, I can't find one.

COURT REPORTER: Aw, c'mon. He always comes back to court. He can't get enough.

BENCH: What was that?

COURT REPORTER: I said the Reverend Rogers always comes back to court. He loves it. Anyone who's been around this place knows that.

BENCH: Would you put that on the record?

COURT REPORTER: In the sixteen years I have worked in this court, I have seen Sugar Rogers many times, and it has been my observation that, when paroled, he returns on the adjourn date to answer the charges against him.

BENCH: Now that is a reason. Paroled on the advice of the court reporter. Give me a two-week date.

BRIDGEMAN: How about 11/5?

BENCH: November 5, in AE-17, upstairs.

D: Sir, every man has his own way of doing things, and I would like to do something for you.

BRIDGEMAN: All right. Keep yours hands at your side.

D: I am drawing this leaf from my Bible, in my breast pocket, and I would like to read it to the court, as a gesture of gratitude for the justice you have shown me.

BENCH: What have you got there, a poem?

D: Yes, your honor. But it's more than a poem. It's a prayer.

BENCH: Well, why don't you just read it to yourself on the way out. Next case, please.

BRIDGEMAN: Recall, Docket Number Y968009, Maurice Eternity, charged with possession of a controlled substance in the seventh degree.

D has crossed toothpicks sticking through his nose and hanging out the nostrils.

BENCH: Well, if you won't take 90 days, I'm holding you on $50 bail, pending the lab report.

D: You go on and do what you're doing, just like you always done. All I had was two vitamin pills. Everything else, I already done time for. You busting my ass on my record, it isn't right. A hundred years ago you would have made me a slave, and that wasn't right, and this here ain't right, either.

DA: Your honor, this defendant has refused to cooperate. During an interview, he spoke in an incomprehensible tongue. Possibly Arabic.

BENCH: How do you know that?

DA: It's in my write-up.

D: I was incomprehensible, that's all you know. Don't say I was speaking Arabic when you don't even know what it sounds like.

LAS: Anyway, I'm requesting a 730.

BENCH: 730 ordered.

D: Your honor, you'll have to speak up. I can't hear what you're saying.

BENCH: Psychiatric examination! Six weeks, please.

D: Aw shit. Ever since I became a follower of the teachings of Elijah Muhammad, I've been going through your damn psychiatric examinations. I believe the white man is the devil, so that makes me crazy, right.

D is a Hasidic Jew; the judge is a religious one. They are the only two people in court wearing eighteenth-century garb. Arrest to arraignment time is a phenomenal six hours flat. On a Friday afternoon, the system wants him out before the newspapers or the Hasidic politicos get word; out before the Sabbath, which falls at sundown.

BENCH: Why is this man in handcuffs?

A/O: Because he kicked the shit out of me when I tried to give him a parking ticket.

PA: Your honor, my client was taking his mother to the hospital. She had had a heart attack and he couldn't find a parking space.

BENCH: Take the handcuffs off, and, gentlemen, step up.

They confer at length. The judge looks at his watch.

BENCH: Now look what we've done. Sundown has passed. He'll have to walk all the way back to Brooklyn. You see, under Jewish law, if an automobile journey is begun in daylight, it can continue into the Sabbath. But if it begins after sundown, it must be on foot. Well, it's too late now.

They confer some more. The audience is not filled with rabbinic scholars. In the front row, a large, fat, bald, bright-pink cop stands up. He looks mean and is wearing heavy motorcycle boots and a black T-shirt that sports a silver eagle over his gut and DEUTSCHLAND *in screaming gothic script across his chest. He is tired of waiting and agitated and cries out.*

P/O: What's taking so long? What is this guy, better than a black man or something?

Madeline Quattlebaum is a senior citizen, otherworldly and very street. She wears black plastic bags on her feet, knotted at the ankle and open-toed; slacks made for a fat man and gathered; and a blouse, missing a sleeve. Her history is of confinement of one kind or another. When the conductor asked her to stop throwing orange peels on the floor of the train, she pulled out a knife and threatened him.

In court, she spoke only through her lawyer and pled guilty for 30 days and was about to go unnoticed.

BENCH: Does the defendant wish to say anything before I impose sentence?

D: You a fool, you antique Confederate motherfucker.

BRIDGEMAN: Docket Number Y970173, Richie Rich, charged with unauthorized use of a motor vehicle— Goddamn it. This ain't no Richie Rich; this is my cousin John. We hung out together and everything. Hey, John, what the hell are you doing here?

D: Hiya, Lock. I got arrested.

BRIDGEMAN: It's been so many years, I've kind of lost touch. What you been up to?

D: I was in the Marines.

BRIDGEMAN: Holy shit, me too, I was in North Carolina.

D: I went everywhere.

BRIDGEMAN: You still living in the old neighborhood?

D: Yeah, same place

BRIDGEMAN: I got to come up there and see you. I was just asking my mother what you were up to, and here you are.

DA: Your honor, the defendant was found asleep in the rear seat of a car.

LAS: May we approach?

BENCH: Come on.

BRIDGEMAN: Anyway, I got two daughters now. Twins. They're not two months old. I guess you'll have to come and see me. I got to stay home and feed the twins.

D: Congratulations.

BRIDGEMAN: Hey, everybody. I'd like you to meet a brother. This is John Hightower. Six or seven years ago, we were really tight, weren't we, John? You know, you ought to be ashamed of yourself, getting busted; but don't feel too bad, sooner or later, everybody comes through here.

LAS: At this time, my client pleads guilty to disorderly conduct, waives formal arraignment, and waives any adjournment for sentencing.

BENCH: Time served.

BRIDGEMAN: Let the record reflect the defendant is handed written notice of his right to appeal within sixty days, in English and Spanish. And don't come back, y'hear?

———

A/O: I'm from the three-two, right in the middle of Harlem. I used to be in the one-ten, then I got laid off. When I come back on, they put me in the three-two. One-ten is out in Queens, real quiet precinct. Your stores and restaurants keep you running around, but it's all bullshit. In the three-two, when you get a collar, it's legitimate. It suits me too, I got a big mortgage to pay.

They say, ever since Joseph Wambaugh, every cop believes he's got a book in him. Not in the one-ten. But in the three-two, well, like last Saturday we got this call—a regular radio run. A bar has a guy passed out cold on the floor, and the place is so crowded they ain't got room for him. My partner picks him up and slaps him around, and he comes to, a little bit, but as soon as we let him go, he falls down again. Then we drag him outside. My partner wants to drag him by the tie, but I was afraid it would strangle him, so we dragged his arms. We get him outside and stand him up, and same thing, over he goes, right into the concrete. So we don't know what to do.

Someone comes over and says he lives around the corner with his sister, so we drag him over there. By this time he's bleeding and everything, and his nose is smashed up. The sister comes to the door and says, "Thanks for bringing him home, fellas." And then she says, "But where's his wheelchair?"

8

"They dropped them leaflets on us in Vietnam," said the ex-Marine court part specialist. "Said, 'Why is the black man fighting this war? Why is the black man always fighting to preserve the system that oppresses him?' Well, I was ready to come home right then, but what could I do? I was in Vietnam, out in the middle of some damn jungle."

9

Howard Hick is small, delicate, doe-like. He is easily influenced and overly impressionable, but he is only sixteen.
Yesterday afternoon he walked into a grocery store, pulled
out a large hunting knife, and demanded the money in the
cash register. The grocer panicked. The machine jammed.
Howard cursed, threatened, and swashbuckled, even tried
to pry it open himself, but the cash drawer was really
stuck.

Howard didn't know what to do. "Oscar give me this
knife and sent me in here, and if I don't come out soon,
he's going to come in here and kill us both. He said he
would, and he's right outside. I got to have the money."

The grocer said he would get the repairman and called
the police. Oscar was arrested as the lookout, and Howard
was caught with the knife in his hand. They are in court together on charges of armed robbery.

Oscar is large and sullen and seventeen. He has nothing
to say. Howard is beaming. When the District Attorney
asks for $20,000 bail on each, his shoulders spread. Yester-
day he was Oscar's punk. Today they are co-defendants.

DA: The People serve statement notice, pursuant to Sec-
tion 710.30 (1A) of the criminal procedure law.
LAS: As to which defendant?
DA: Notice is served on both. Oscar said, "I don't know
nothing. I was just waiting for a bus." And defendant
Howard Hick said, in substance, "Oscar made me do it."

Howard winced, but there was worse to come. Oscar was
held in jail on $2,000. Howard was paroled, being
underage and a first arrest. Paroled into the custody of his
angry parents, who took him home and gave him a good
licking.

In the morning, the whole neighborhood will hear that the graceful shrimp who shadowed Oscar is no more. He has tangled with the law, and you better stay out of his way, because, from now on, Howard Hick is bad.

His sweet little face is enough to make you smile, which the whole neighborhood will do. Only the criminal justice system will legitimatize his evil and give him the strength to act on it.

In slave times, the horn was a military voice, used to call and direct troops above the din of battle. A horn in the hands of a slave was criminal possession of a dangerous instrument, a Class D felony. One of America's principal contributions to Western music is the extension and mastery of the horn, accomplished by black musicians, descendants of slaves.

Because it was feared that they would read Abolitionist pamphlets and forge papers with which to escape, literate slaves were outlawed. Teaching a slave to read and write was a Class B misdemeanor. Slaves organized clandestine schools and had a higher literacy rate than the poor whites of the time. When they were freed, education was their first and most persistent demand. And throughout a history lacking leisure, black America has produced an astonishing tradition of literature and scholarship.

Today, carrying a knife is a Class D felony. But even if it's only a flick knife or a dagger, there must be a valid search. Which means: it's only a knife if it's in plain view. In the ghetto, the fashion among male youths is to wear a big folding knife in the back pocket, with as much of it showing as you dare.

Where authority is feared, denying it will always show strength. Where authority is cruel, denying it will always show bravery. And where authority is confused, ambivalent, embarrassed, and all the rest, beating it is often the only satisfaction left.

Hungry people do not dream of the next meal they so

badly need; they dream of a chauffeur-driven limousine, with a bar in the back, and a telephone in case they have to talk to their baby when they're on the open road. Hungry people dream of release. Rebirth.

Oppressed peoples cannot help admiring ther own nihilists. Despair is always a conservative force. By the time he is grown, Howard Hick won't be funny.

10

The Police Department is about 7½ percent black and Hispanic, but the federal courts have ordered it to hire more minorities, and it is complying. When despair turns angry, a handful of the most desperate are hired to police the rest, or, as Vaughan sees it, "They think it makes a difference to us to get clubbed over the head by a black cop instead of a white cop. That's their idea of progress."

11

One morning Charles came in with his forehead wrinkled.

"Last night," he said, "there was these two guys went into a social club. They paid $10 apiece to get in, and when they got inside, the bartender refused to serve them on account of they wasn't members. So they got mad and went home. When they cooled off, they went back, you know, polite and everything, but the cops were waiting there. And, um . . . Well, they was my mother's brothers."

"Talk to the DA on the case," I said.

"I already seen her."

Later in the day, the case was called in AT-1. Charles stood right next to the prosecutor, rocking back on his heels. "This ain't nothing," he whispered across to his uncles, "just misdemeanors."

The co-defendants were paroled on consent of the People. Their case was worth almost nothing, but they didn't know it. "Ain't that boy of Mildred's something," they said. "I guess they got to let you go when you got a nephew right up there in court."

Kitty learned to track cases in the computer, watching out for her constituents. She offered to teach Charles. In fact, they all know how to use the computer terminals and keep the family posted. It isn't just checking off boxes anymore. Court part specialists are legal advisers. In their lives and in their families, they are the Political Connection. This is a good job.

12

"The church is in Jamaica, Queens, but the party is up in Harlem," both Charles and his wedding invitations boasted. So on the date I was up and traveling early, in my best clothes.

On my way to the subway, I passed a man coming out of an insurance company in full combat dress. Boots, fatigues, gloves, and a beret, with pliers and files hanging from his belt, and on his back a big nylon knapsack filled to a crushing weight. It was Clarence Commando, burglar. I remembered him from court, dressed the same way, only the knapsack was empty. I nodded, said hello, and he nodded back.

A long walk, two sweaty train rides, change for the bus, and I was at the church, damp and wrinkled from the border crossing. Charles's mother kissed me, thanked me for coming, and said she knew who I was. His cousin ushered me to the row reserved for friends from work. Nobody else was sitting there.

Charles's family is old Harlem, but they had always been poor until Charles went to college and got a good job.

His family is very proud of him, and today he is marrying, upwardly mobile.

Rita, the bride, is the daughter of a dentist and an only child. She has never been poor and is used to the best, which her delighted parents feel Charles can provide.

So no effort was spared. Banks of flowers, a full choir, six bridesmaids, a maid of honor, a flower girl, and a little boy in a tweed suit with short pants, carrying a velvet pillow with the ring on it.

The groom was resplendent in white tie and tails, like a tap dancer from Hollywood. The bride was in antique silk and pearls, shy, innocent, and dignified.

The congregation was hushed. The mothers gasped and couldn't fan themselves. The young girls had tears in their eyes, and everyone breathed deeply.

But for the disagreement between the choirmaster and the organist, who eye each other throughout the hymns, everything went slowly, formal and precise. So rehearsed and so important. No one moved or spoke in the motions of real life.

The couple said "I do," and kissed, and led the procession back down the aisle. Charles mugged for the cameras and played to the crowd. The basketball star, most comfortable with everyone watching.

Outside the church, the mother of the bride swooned, pegged me, and said, "You have to excuse me. I'm a little bit meshugga today." Then the bridal party got into a fleet of Cadillacs and sped away, with horns tooting "Here Comes the Bride." And on to Harlem.

Coming out of the subway, I followed a blind man, whose seeing-eye dog had a cast on its leg. The street itself twinkled, covered with a fine layer of broken glass. A little girl passed and said, "Welcome to Harlem, mister," but with a puzzled look. When the light at the corner turned green, a motorcycle hoodlum dressed in leather screeched through the intersection with his front wheel a foot off the ground, leaving a backwash of debris from which the head of a white doll rolled across my path. I was a little nervous.

A cop approached a man sitting on a porch. The man was shouting, "But I live here. Upstairs. This is my home. It may not look like much to you, but it's the only home I got. And if I can't sit here on a part of my own home, where can I sit?"

I watched my feet and walked on to the Celebrity Club. Historic old jazz joint with Charles's name on the bulletin board. Inside, there were art-deco murals of dogs racing, columns wound with wired paper vines, and a wedding party in progress. A clique of court part specialists was gathered at the edge of the dancing. I joined them immediately.

The disco blared, the liquor flowed, the fat of fried chicken dripped, ashes fell into champagne, and cake frosting smudged across brand-new neckties. The bouquet was thrown. Polaroids—to be passed around the office— were snapped. And pretty young girls took turns wearing out old men on the dance floor. The groom's mother's brothers, their case dismissed (complaining witness declines to prosecute), whirled effectively while Charles's oldest uncle hurt his back jitterbugging, and the bride's mother dipped her ostrich-feather hat into the punch without it coming off her head.

The bridal couple left to catch a jet to Disneyworld for the honeymoon, and soon after the court part specialists ordered three taxis and went farther uptown, to the projects, for a private party at Kitty's.

The party was nonstop dancing. At one point, Kitty mounted a footstool and yelled, "Somebody grab me, I don't care who!" before plunging into the crowd. Being a gentleman and close at hand, I grabbed. Later, her mother, who is a religious woman, relented, shouting, "I'll dance, but I don't grind."

To everyone's surprise, Vaughan was the best dancer.

They said it didn't fit his work personality. "Well, you finally made it," he said to me, "up in Harlem. In the projects. You probably the first white person ever been to a party here. But you work in black misery. It's about time you saw yourself a little black fun."

I couldn't resist the family photo album, and Kitty's mother commented. Just like Vaughan's, it went all the way back to great-great-great-somebody dressed in Civil War uniform. Already American when photography was invented.

When the night was almost gone, Kitty's mother taught us the Stroll and other dances of her day, and fed us breakfast. Then Kitty walked us to the subway. We said goodbye, and Kitty said to Vaughan's date, "Next boyfriend, get a car."

As we waited for the train, Vaughan looked at the crowd and said, "This isn't right. All these black people out here in the middle of the night. Black people need more discipline. Need more self-control—"

"And white people need more spontaneity," I added.

Riding the A train through Harlem in the middle of the night, I felt protected by Charles's fate. All I could think of were the stories my mother told me about the good times Jews used to have; about the weddings when she was young and poor and oppressed in a Polish ghetto.

At 125th Street we all changed trains and went our separate ways, and I got back into my white fear.

CHAPTER SEVEN

1

With Christians hoping for the crystalline purity of snow, heaven sent freezing rain and filthy sludge as more appropriate. It is Christmas at the courthouse.

The busy season starts with the coming of cold weather. Time for meat and potatoes, back-to-school overcoats, and baby needs a new pair of shoes; money is needed more urgently, and those without take greater risks to get it. These needs culminate at Christmas. Without money, Christmas in New York is No Christmas. No celebration, no indulgence, and no way to pretend that life is generous, even for one ritual day. People will do rather ugly things to be able to have Christmas, and when they can't, they do crazy things. Potential collars abound.

Christmas is also when the cops need their overtime

money most. And while it's cold and frantic outside, it's warm and cozy at the courthouse.

So it's ready cases piled high in AT-1. High-speed arraignment and no recess, while the backlog builds toward the holy day.

2

In the cold, the bums flock to AT-1 and form a solid block in the last few rows. Even in number, they are no trouble to anyone, except as they reveal lives devoid of expectation. In pristine corridors upstairs, sophisticated senior citizens shop the Supreme Court calendars for interesting trials. For the bums, arraignments are good enough. The heat alone makes it interesting.

"Hey, bub," says one old fart, elbowing his sidekick in the ribs, "don't you know there's no sleeping allowed in this court."

Two new court officers have come to AT-1. They are both dark-skinned and will replace two white guys who are being promoted to Supreme Court the first of the year.

They're supposed to be getting acclimated. It's a terrible time to be new on the job. With everyone trying to be Christmas-cheerful, they have to stand around like blank strangers.

One of them is big and mean-looking. He's the new part captain. He wears mirrored aviator glasses, which he never takes off, and low black shitkicker boots. His uniform is patched and ragged, with a shiny seat and threads hanging out of every hem. They say he worked night court in Brooklyn for seven years. Morose. Quiet, maybe even enlightened. I don't believe he can see anything through those shades in this dingy light, but I'm afraid to ask. They say his name is Jim.

The other is a raw recruit. He's young, short, and care-free. His name is Mr. Slice. He wears 49-cent transparent toy sunglasses with fingerprints all over the lenses.

Mr. Slice seems to take no interest in his job and mostly wanders around the back of the courtroom, munching a Baby Ruth candy bar, with the wrapper peeled down like a banana, making it last all afternoon. He is unusually kind to the audience. He never yells or throws anybody out. And even under stress, he always appears to be reasonable and peaceful.

He nods a lot, probably sheer agreeability, and he falls asleep at every break in the record, as if he knows the ropes by instinct.

Vaughan knows him from the projects and says I have misjudged him entirely. However, he is the only uniformed court officer who could ever be mistaken for a defendant. I find myself scanning the back of his hands for needle tracks, even though he's in uniform.

3

When the court part specialists were finally given their piece of the long-awaited, retroactive, citywide pay raise, Kitty shouted at me. "What's wrong with you? You're getting a check for $960 retroactive and $60 a week in your hand after that—"

"Don't even tell him about it, Kitty," Vaughan said. "You know how evil and oppressive he sees the system. He finds out they paying him more money, he might jump out a window on the fifteenth floor."

Kitty is using her new income to move to another apartment. Brand-new. "Nobody ever lived there before," she says proudly. "So when you put the lights on, you don't have to see no little brown brothers running around, because if there's one thing I hate, it's cockroaches."

Even at work, Kitty appeared to be doing well until she worked night court the night they arraigned the two white doctors who threw eggs in the face of the mayor. They were protesting the closing of their hospital, but the mayor took it personally. A bureau chief came down to do the arraignment himself. When he asked for $10,000 bail on family men with no previous record, gainfully employed as medical doctors, Kitty burst out laughing and asked how much he would want if the eggs had been hard-boiled.

It got a laugh, and nothing more was said at the time, but since then, the whole chain of command called Kitty into its private office, one link at a time, and reprimanded her.

"I told them I couldn't help it. You ask for $10,000 on a case like that and it's funny. So I laughed. So what? I told them they could write me up, ruin my career, do whatever they gotta do, but quit bothering me. I already laughed. I can't take it back. It's done. And then they give me all this bullshit about teamwork and loyalty, and that's what I really can't stand."

Now she'll probably never be a supervisor.

4

Lockheed was going down the drain with his marriage. Frequent absence, chronic lateness, an unkempt appearance, and what-did-I-do-wrong written all over his face.

One morning he announced, "That's it. It's over. I'm finished. You're looking at a bum. I got no home, no place to go, no clothes, nothing. She threw me out."

"Literally, or she asked you to leave?" Vaughan inquired scientifically.

"We had a fight. An argument. No punching, but a little bit of pushing and shoving, and I walked out. When I came back, she wouldn't open the damn door."

"I've been there myself," Vaughan said.

"Last night I stayed at my brother's house. He says it's cool with him, but I don't know what to do. I like a hard mattress and my brother's bed is soft. I like a hard pillow too, and everything I own is over there. My papers, my shirts . . . my children."

"Wait a day and call her up," Vaughan said.

"Yeah, that's what I figured," said Lockheed. "It was my fault, really. We were arguing before dinner, and I got so mad I couldn't eat. I wanted pork chops, and she wanted to cook chicken. But she made the pork. Made it fast, and cooked it solid, too . . ."

"And you wouldn't eat it?"

"I told her to shove it up her ass. I don't know why."

When he called the next day, there was no answer. He went back and found the apartment empty. His wife had taken the twins to her mother's house. She left a note saying to send child-support money there.

All Lock wants for Christmas is a war. He's willing to pay his own fare over, and bring his own weapons.

5

In Russia, where the legal system prides itself on no bullshit and exact sensitivity in the administration of human relationships, all anger is seen as disease.

Political prisoners are not punished in Russia but treated with distance and remoteness. In confinement, the torture function is a sensual, personal thing, while being ignored is a denial of humanity. The Russians consider paying no attention the ultimate sophistication of torture.

In the Serbsky Forensic Psychiatric Hospital in Moscow, political dissidents struggle to prove their sanity, while thieves, murderers, and embezzlers energetically fake all manner of irrationality to preserve their status as certified madmen. Every criminal has the secret ambition to be pronounced officially irresponsible, especially in Russia, where they enjoy better food, softer beds, and the peace of hospital life. Under such conditions, the desire for sanity, which leads to labor camps, really is crazy, proving the state correct.

This keeps the criminal justice system clean, professional, and orderly, but the mental hospitals of Russia are bursting.

Here in America, we do the opposite. Especially at Christmas.

6

WRITE-UP: D broke arm falling through glass door of gas station after assaulting pump jockey and P/O.
D: Your honor, I'm asking $5 million for my broken arm. Cash money now, I don't want no check.
BENCH: 730, psychiatric examination ordered . . .

BRIDGEMAN: Docket Number Y972861, Economy Collins, charged with 165.45, 140.35, and 110/155.25. Collins. Economy Collins. Step on it, mister, we haven't got all day!
The defendant is calm but slow. When he reaches the table, he snaps to attention. His trousers are synthetic, powder blue. He has on a powder-blue sweatshirt and broken black-framed glasses. There is hair only on the top of his head, the sides and back are shaved. In his hand is a powder-blue cap.
A/O: I caught him with a bunch of credit cards down at the bank, playing with the automatic machines. I observed him for about fifteen minutes, and then I arrested him.
LAS: Mr. Collins, the court is going to ask you some questions. You will have to answer them as truthfully as you can.

BENCH: Mr. Collins, do you know where you are?

D: Yes.

BENCH: Where? Please tell me.

D: I am in Court AT-1, in the city of New York.

BENCH: Hmm . . . And do you know who I am?

D: Yes.

BENCH: Well, answer as soon as I ask. Who am I?

D: You are the Honorable John Jay, Justice of the Court.

A/O: Gee whiz. I didn't even know the answer to that one.

BENCH: Mr. Collins, why are you here?

D: I was brought here in innocence.

BENCH: Well, sir, it is the fundamental principle of our judicial system that no man shall ever have to prove his innocence. If you are not guilty, you will be so judged, but I am not here to examine the merits of the case. Now, guilty or innocent, do you understand the charges that are being lodged against you?

D: They're all lies.

BENCH: They may be lies, they may be truth, but do you understand what those charges are?

D: Of course not. I'm innocent of all charges.

BENCH: Mr. Collins, we are too busy to play games here. I'm going to ask you some more questions and you're going to answer them. Got it?

D: (nods).

BENCH: Mr. Collins, what do you do for a living?

D: I create.

BENCH: What do you create?

D: Creations.

BENCH: Like what?

D: Like anything.

BENCH: Be specific, please.

D: I can't. I created the whole world.

BENCH: When was that?

D: A long time ago.

BENCH: Can you be exact?

D: I can't remember. It was billions of years ago.

BENCH: Are you God, Mr. Collins?

D: Yes.

BENCH: Now what about these credit cards? They weren't yours, were they? And you did not have permission or authority to possess them, did you?

D: They are mine!

BENCH: Mr. Collins, are you also known as Schlomo Rabinowitz of Bayonne, New Jersey?

D: Yes.

BENCH: And are you also Miriam Riderielli?

D: Yes.

BENCH: And I suppose John Jay too?

D: Of course.

BENCH: I'm ordering a civil commit.

BRIDGEMAN: Officer, you'll have to take him up there yourself. Wait for the papers.

A/O: Hey, Economy, where you going? Take a seat on the bench with the angels.

BRIDGEMAN: Docket Number Y975455, Francine Rabbledoux, charged with arson and burglary, both felonies.

This is her third trip to court since summer. She used to look like a small-town housewife. Page-boy hair, pointy glasses, and a stay-pressed pants suit. She was, in fact, a housewife from New England. Then she came to New York, got a job as a cashier in a porno movie house, and ran off with the cashbox two hours later, right into the arms of a cop. She tried to represent herself in court, but they dismissed the case and over her argument shouted, "Go back to Massachusetts." Instead, she went out and did it again, and was sent for a psychiatric examination.

Now she doesn't look so ordinary. Her hair is singed into a pixie cut, and the skin on her face is peeling off as if it were sunburned. Her hands are wrapped in gauze, and her teeth are clenched.

She is charged with breaking and entering a closed porno theater with a pail full of gasoline and a match. The gasoline splashed as she lit it. There was extensive damage to the balcony, and she was four days in the prison infirmary before her fingers had healed enough to be printed.

BENCH: An excellent attorney is standing beside you. Why not avail yourself of his experience and training?

D: I'm sorry; for what I have to say to this court, an attorney is not appropriate.

BENCH: The right to counsel is a valuable right.

D: I know.

LAS: She's an evangelist, your honor.

D: I am not an evangelist. I am a messenger of Christ.

BENCH: When did he start giving you messages?

D: My instruction comes in a form this court would not understand.

BENCH: I'm ordering a psychiatric examination.

D: But I've just come back from a psychiatric examination.

LAS: Your honor, I object. This defendant was found fit in November.

BENCH: Objection noted; 730 ordered.

The offer is an A misdemeanor and one year in jail. The defendant wants to take it, if only he might have a chance to speak to his wife.

BENCH: Absolutely not. We have neither the architectural provisions nor the staff for such a visit. It is not allowed.

The defendant pleads guilty anyway, and they leave him on the bench. Tears stream down his face. Out in the audience his wife is crying, too.

With no announcement, Big Jim slides two chairs across the court and places them on opposite sides of the little wall. Then he beckons the defendant and his wife.

BENCH: All right. But no touching, and keep it brief, please.

The defendant and his wife lock in embrace, and Big

Jim turns his back. Half an hour later the defendant goes off to do his time with every eye in the room following him.

BENCH: What's the matter with everybody?

COURT REPORTER: We are not donkeys.

A/O: Andrew, you got carfare home?

D: I'll get it from the Legal Aid, thanks anyway. And thanks for all you've done. Take care of yourself, man.

A/O: You too.

CO-D: How can you thank that man? He just got through busting you.

D: Look, sonny. I've been going to jail since 1963. Some cops don't take their foot out of your ass from the moment they grab you until you get to the judge. But this guy treated me right. He explained his game to me. Made a few phone calls for me, and he even got me some cigarettes. And when you been around like I have, you know the difference.

The defendant is white. His head is shaved, his pupils dilated, and he is brought to the bridge in handcuffs, wearing a white robe. Some kind of Krishna worshipper. Last night he was observed trying to burn down the temple. Today he refuses to give a name or be printed.

BRIDGEMAN: Docket Number Y988999, John Doe. Charged with 150.15, arson.

BENCH: Look up at me when I talk to you.

D: You don't have to look at a man to know when he's talking.

BENCH: Okay, look down, then. But I suggest you tell me your name, right now.

D: I don't like that suggestion.

With a squeak from the side door, the court reporter curses silently and still tries to sneak back to his post unnoticed.

D: Who the hell is that guy? He has no right to be here! He's laughing at me, I can tell!

BENCH: Hey, where have you been? You can't walk off like that while we're holding court.

COURT REPORTER: When nature calls, I must answer.

D: You see what I mean. See the way he looks at me.

BENCH: It's strictly administrative and not your concern, sir. We'll begin all over again.

COURT REPORTER: This is the first time anything like this has ever happened to me.

BENCH: Are you aware of the charges against you?

D: Ha ha.

BENCH: Do you know who I am?

D: You're the guy who sits up high and asks questions.

BENCH: And who are you?

D: I am the final judge.

BENCH: Put him in, I'm ordering a 730.

D (*to A/O*): Take a walk, fat man.

Officer Lockheed, guarding the rail, snaps to attention, salutes the judge, and moves to parade rest. Then back to attention.

UCO: Corporal Lockheed, present sir. Combat ready.

As the judge takes note, Officer Lockheed unhooks his tie and unbuttons his tunic and shirt. Underneath is a Marine Corps T-shirt saying COMBAT READY.

UCO: We want a war. We want a war. That's what they taught me in the Marines. Too young for 'Nam and too early for the next one, but I'm ready. I just got to go.

BENCH: Officer, while I admire your indignation, I am not sure you are fully informed of the difficulties engendered by your view.

UCO: No, sir. We got to teach the world they can't fuck with us.

BENCH: Perhaps we can discuss this later.

———

BRIDGEMAN: Arf Wilson. Return on warrants. Docket Numbers Y730304 and Y818276, charged with . . .

When called, the defendant rises, leans on his cane, and makes his way to the bridge. The computer says he is fifty-two, but he looks ninety. In between his gasps and groans, he insists he is okay and can make it.

A court officer with a chair rushes in from behind just as he collapses. The arrest report says he has tattoos on arms, thighs, and penis. Everyone is hoping he won't die.

BENCH: What were the charges on those warrants? I'm afraid I didn't hear it right.

BRIDGEMAN: Two counts of 205.10, escape in the second degree.

BENCH: That's what I have. What is this, some kind of joke?

DA: No, your honor. While on a bank stakeout, this officer was panhandled by the defendant and recognized him from a previous arrest.

BENCH: Are you asking for bail?

DA: Your honor, in 1977, while awaiting trial for petty larcency, this defendant developed tremors and was placed in Columbia Presbyterian Hospital, from which he escaped by requesting to go to his Alcoholics Anonymous meeting and eluding the officer who took him. And in 1978, while awaiting arraignment on a grand larceny auto, he had a heart attack and escaped from the intensive care unit.

WRITE-UP: While practicing the church organ, CW observed D taking the crucifix, running around the pulpit, and tapping it against the floor. When CW returned with priest, the cross was gone. Two days later, CW spotted D in congregation. Cops called. Apprehended in vicinity by Radio Motor Patrol car. Cross recovered.

PA: Your honor, my client has a Ph.D. degree in psychology. He is an author and has a private practice. Is it

all right if I call him doctor on the record?
BENCH: Counselor, you call him whatever you think will help him.

The defendant is very white and academic—tweed jacket, silk tie, button-down collar. And very anxious. His report says he is a transvestite, and there are seven prior arrests for assault, kidnapping, homicide, and manslaughter.

DA: I want to read the complaint into the record because the bizarre and serious nature of this crime should be reflected in the bail.

PA: I object.

BENCH: I got the complaint right here. I'm reading it.

THE COMPLAINT: . . . did willfully tie her up with a rope, whip her with a belt, drop hot wax on her feet, place clamps on her breasts, and beat her at gunpoint, and also place a pistol in her anus and vagina . . .

The defendant is a young woman beautiful in the most voluptuous ways. Sloppy jeans and a flimsy T-shirt hide little. All rolling curves and grace, her body radiates, while her face looks vacant and disconnected.

The defendant is mentally retarded. She has a long record of violence, confinement, and escape. She is here for sexually assaulting her female cousin, who is also retarded.

Her worried father is here from California, her weary brother from Delaware. They join the bench conference and agree to send her to a private hospital. The cop agrees to clear her with Corrections and take her there.

As she enters, the prisoners in the crowded feeder pens fall silent. They stare at her and reach out between the bars. As she passes, she touches every outstretched hand. The last cell is vacant but for a man in the front corner with no shirt and his pants down. His hands are cuffed behind him and he is trying to masturbate with his thighs. She stops, then reaches down and pats him on the head, as if she were a child and he a newborn fawn.

7

Sitting in the little room at the back, we have returned temporarily to our normal state of rest. The rush is on, and cases are piling up, but FAX, the fingerprint computer, is down. The system must wait. The court reporter is asleep, and Officer Lockheed is sitting at the desk, comatose, with his head wrapped in the sports pages. Beside me, Big Jim sits motionless. There's no telling where he is, except maybe by the length of the ash hanging from his cigarette. As it falls into his pocket, I know he is out.

8

The court officers' Christmas party was held in a jury part. There was no food, but lots of beer and whiskey. They brought in a couple of hookers and a Polaroid camera, and took turns photographing one another on top. There was only one fight, in which a court bench was broken. And one injury. A holstered gun went off into the floor and sent marble chips into the foot of a poor fool who thought he had shot himself. At which point someone pointed out that carrying a gun provided a totally false sense of security.

The court reporters' party was the most lavish. Fish pastes, molded Jell-O, and even ham with pineapple rings, just in case anyone forgot that they make three times as much money as anyone but the cops and lawyers.

Then there was the clerks' party, the Legal Aid function, and a cops' party sponsored by the transit police. And others. There was one at the end of every day.

In the halls, the rich prostitutes' lawyers handed out little bottles of perfume to all the women, and cigars and ball-point pens to the men, making us feel almost as if we had influence to peddle. I went wherever I was invited. It was nice, but after a while I didn't distinguish between a ceremonial shot of whiskey in the judges' chambers and checking off the boxes. It's all the same mask.

Whatever is wrong in life seems most wrong at Christmas.

9

"I remember one year, I didn't have no Christmas," Vaughan said. "I must have been around ten or eleven years old. On Christmas Eve my mother was coming home with all her presents. They pulled a knife on her and snatched her purse, and took all our presents, too. And we didn't have nothing.

"And you be down in AT-1, watching them plead to petit larceny and get a conditional discharge, and go free. And you feel sorry for them."

10

Down in AT-1, Judge Woof was sitting, although he hadn't arrived yet, and appearing for the People, Ms. Bopp. Ms. Bopp is thin, curvy, sexy, feisty, feminist, and tall enough to play pro basketball; extremely attractive, even if she is a prosecutor.

"Thank God you're here today. I need your help," she said.

"Who me?" I asked, thrilled.

"You've got to save me from Woof."

"Save you?" I asked, astonished. "You must be kidding. He's the most thoughtful, learned, and serious of them all. He worries and cares more than anyone. He's so good, he'll save you from yourself."

"He is not," she said. "He's a terrible egomaniac who wants the whole world to love him. He wants to be every-

body's uncle. It's crazy. He paroles these monsters, and
they terrorize the community. He doesn't care who or
what they destroy, as long as he can flatter his own ego."

"But it's Christmas. Where is your heart?"

"Howard," she said coyly, "you're not helping."

Just then Judge Woof came in. He shook the wet off his
coat and looked at Ms. Bopp as if he wished he was shaking
the slush right into her face.

"Good morning, Counselor," he said to her coldly, then
turned to me with a smile. "Have you seen the *Law Journal* yet?"

"Why, no," I said. "I find the *Law Journal* incomprehensible."

"Here," he said, "take my copy. I've already finished
with it. Go in the back and have a coffee and look at it.
Enjoy it."

"Thanks for the tip."

I looked at Ms. Bopp, and then at the *Law Journal.* The
day proved slow. The cops had already received their last
overtime checks before Christmas and were home with
their families. The cases were few and simple. The fireworks between judge and prosecutor never went off, and
neither did my political emergence as their go-between.
With Ms. Bopp, who was young and new to the system and
still believed in it, I said the wrong things and got nowhere. By afternoon, everyone was just waiting around for
their respective parties to begin.

AT-1 would have closed early but for one case. A mandatory youth offender, represented by Mr. Dart, who spent
forever interviewing him in the back and making phone
calls, and who would not be rushed.

"That son-of-a-bitch," said the bridgeman. "I'm gonna
miss my party on account of him. Dart's playing games
again. He could have been done an hour ago."

"Don't be upset," said the judge. "It isn't even four
o'clock. You'll still get out early."

"I'm going back there and drag him out. This shit isn't fair. This is not a Supreme Court appeal, this is an arraignment. How much time does he need?"

"A man's liberty is at stake," said the judge, "and we are all paid to stay until six o'clock. But, Officer, let me give you a bit of personal advice. Mr. Dart is a sensitive and intelligent young man. Too much so for this system. It has made him so hateful and so frustrated that he is now reduced to creating roadblocks and nuisance wherever he can. Any response we show to that will only aggravate it."

"I don't care," said the bridgeman. "I just want to get out of here. It's Christmas."

"Never mind. Mr. Dart is on the verge of a nervous breakdown, which this court will not encourage. Go back there and observe him. See how he's doing, but don't attempt to engage him in any conversation, please. I order you. We must be patient."

The bridgeman huffed off, but quickly returned, announcing, "He's ready."

Mr. Dart entered, blushing, with his jaws locked. Ms. Bopp perked up. The judge looked terrible. The defendant looked like the kind of kid you see in the front row of an outdoor Mozart festival with a book of poetry in his back pocket.

BRIDGEMAN: Docket Number Y989574. Brian Warme, charged with robbery and possession of a weapon, both felony counts.

LAS: Your honor, I know this is a serious case, but it is not what it appears. My client is an honor student.

BENCH: Excuse me, Mr. Dart, but I'll hear the People's application first, as is customary.

DA: Thank you, your honor. This is a gunpoint robbery of an elderly woman in Riverside Park. A positive identification was made, and a loaded weapon was recovered, I think.

LAS: You think?

DA: Officer, it says that the gun was thrown into the bushes. Was it recovered?

A/O: That's what the old lady told us, but when we searched him at the precinct, we found a loaded pistol in his underpants.

DA: A loaded gun was recovered, your honor. We're asking $5,000.

LAS: Your honor, my client is seventeen years old. He lives at home with his family. He has no prior felony record. He is an honor student in his last year at Benjamin Franklin High School. He is extremely gifted. He speaks Latin, Greek, Hebrew, and several modern languages. He has a scholarship to the University of California for next year. He has a whole life and future before him, and I am asking for his parole to preserve that.

BENCH: Please step up.

The bench conference is long. The courtroom is empty, except for the defendant's girlfriend, two sisters, an aunt, and his mother. They are introduced to the conference one at a time, and go back to the audience resigned. But Mr. Dart presses on.

LAS: Your honor, we cannot subject a young man like this to the environment of jail. You know what can happen to him there. Now, if you won't parole him on the basis of his community roots, represented by his family being here, then I am asking that we arrange a special agreement. I have been in touch with a representative of the Andrew Glover Youth Foundation, who is willing to come down here and will agree to stay in constant touch with this defendant and advise the court immediately of any problems, as a condition of parole—

BENCH: I'm sorry, Counselor. A loaded gun on a senior citizen. I can't in conscience grant parole. Can the family make any bail at all?

DA: Your honor, what about the severity of the charges?
LAS: Out of the question. I'm buying them dinner myself.
But if it's acceptable to you, your honor, I'd like to take
personal responsibility for returning my client to court. I'll
have him phone me twice a day and report to you personally, as a condition of parole—
BENCH: Can they make $100?
LAS: Your honor, I'll call him every hour if you want. Or
any other personal assurance that you can think of. Any
condition, as a condition of parole.
BENCH: No, I'm sorry.

*The judge shakes his head. Mr. Dart puts his down on the
bridge, resting it on his hands. Then he pushes his glasses
up to his eyes, looks back at the family, and whispers to his
client, who nods vigorously.*

BENCH: Counselors, I think you better step up again.
DA: I don't believe this. He's going to wind up paroling this
kid. It's almost like telling him to go out and do it again.
Hey, where do you think you're going?
CPS: To the DA's Christmas party.

11

Up on the seventh floor, the halls were filled with prosecu-
tors, drinking and commiserating, with steady streams of
people arriving, milling about, and leaving. Not much apparent cheer, but an awful lot of whiskey.

A distinguished assistant district attorney had his vest
unbuttoned and his spectacles off. He took a big sip of his
drink and placed his arm on my shoulder. "I look around
this room and see three hundred people gathered here who
are probably responsible for more misery, suffering, and
deprivation than any other group this size, anywhere."

I nodded.

"Yesterday," he said, "I suppose because of Christmas, I

consented to parole on an assault case. And last night, he beat up my witness so bad they're not even sure she is going to live. I feel completely responsible."

I clapped him on the back and moved on, edging my way in.

The furniture had all been cleared away. The lights were off, and the staff was all dressed up, smelling of cologne, dancing to the music.

For us, it was the best day's work of the year. Free bar, free music, and getting paid. It was the golden moment of saturnalia, when the common comes into fashion and the young beauties who want to marry lawyers go home instead with the maids and the messenger boys.

The bosses danced, too, and flirted outrageously, but they had devoted their adolescence to something else, and couldn't cut loose.

A high-ranking official whom I hadn't seen since our handshake on my first day shook and shimmied across the floor, while his subordinates laughed. From the darkness, a hand pointed him out. "That's the one I was telling you about. That's the fool took a wrong turn in the basement looking for Records and wound up in the psychiatric pens. He never showed his I.D. or nothing. They gave him a bologna sandwich and he ate it. He was down there six hours under observation, until somebody went and got him. That's him right there."

I saw Ms. Bopp come in, looking crushed, and rushed to get her a drink. Mr. Dart got Brian Warme paroled. She was in no mood for a golden moment of saturnalia.

"Sometimes I feel like going back to Memphis," she said. "At least in Memphis you can lock somebody up and keep him there. Here it doesn't seem worth the effort. You never get anywhere."

"What do you mean?" I said. "The jails of New York are overcrowded. Rikers Island is about to burst. They put away so many people, they've run out of room."

"Oh, no," she said. "They could pack them in like sardines if they wanted to."

After a while, they started playing Latin music, and the black people complained. So they stopped, and the Latins complained. The liquor was all gone anyway. The lights came on. Everyone blinked at the glare. Someone's brand-new leather overcoat had been stolen. Women couldn't find their purses. I had a headache. The party was over.

Outside, it was snowing. Big, picture-book flakes. As I came past the courthouse, the prearraignment sergeant stood without a coat on the steps. He is in charge of all the cops at the courthouse, and the kind of brush-cut spit-shined, starched, pressed militarist that I avoid. I had never spoken to him before (or since for that matter), but it was Christmas. Breathing alcohol, he embraced me and said, "I don't want to be supercop. I don't want to destroy anybody. If I wanted to hurt people, I would never have become a cop. I want to help."

"Merry Christmas, Sergeant," I said. Then he went back to court.

In the morning, I had a hangover and Kitty shouted at me because I had left my turnarounds in court. I couldn't believe that she was serious, but she carried on, calling me all kinds of things, including "chicken-shit baboon." Even after I brought the papers up she yelled.

12

For the concentration-camp survivor who placed his hands against the buttocks of three women while the big Christmas tree at Rockefeller Center was being lit by the President—

For the heart surgeon who threw his ex-wife's color TV out her ninth-floor apartment window and assaulted two cops—

For the seventy-eight-year-old man caught taking bets in the toilet of a state-run betting parlor—

For the young woman carrying a pamphlet by Karl Marx who went into a luxury lobby and unscrewed one light bulb—

For the two teenagers who passed a hash pipe in a car, in plain view of a cop retiring at the end of the year and in need of overtime to pad his pension consideration—

For the eighty-two-year-old guy whose wife wouldn't let him go hunting upstate, so he emptied one barrel of his shotgun out the window and the other at the cop who came in response, and had to be arraigned with a ball of wire holding his hand in traction because the cop shot back—

And for all the random special cases that make this season in the system what it is—

We pray for peace and fulfillment.

Amen.

CHAPTER EIGHT

1

The new year brings the cold and dead of winter. The streets are deserted. There is no one to arrest, and the cops are all in court, under subpoena, giving testimony at the hearings and trials of their abundant Christmas collars. No time for new arrests. AT-1 is at ebb tide.

Nothing's come in but the bums, and a Nazi of sorts. He wore thick glasses and a uniform of Boy Scout issue, with the badges torn off. A strip of bedsheet and a swastika of black electrical tape made his armband. All he did was sit and grin. Word came down not to arrest him and not to annoy him, we don't want a lawsuit over this. But they took him in the back for questioning, and he left. He returned, dressed in nondescript sport clothes and a skull cap crocheted with the Star of David. This time he stayed in the halls telling Jewish lawyers that a gang of Nazis was marching on the courthouse. Crowds gathered at the door, but no one was there.

In this season of taking stock and reconsideration, in these times of grim sophistication, in this place where next year will be last year and before is after, AT-1 is pending ready matters, and finding too much time on its hands.

2

Sometimes the peace gets so captivating I have to escape. Through the park and left at the church, I follow the stone wall lined with garbage. Above the soggy bags and stench, repeating signs read CHURCH PROPERTY. NO DUMPING OF GARBAGE. VIOLATORS WILL BE PROSECUTED TO THE FULL EX- TENT OF THE LAW.

Across the intersection where the wall ends is a pinball parlor. A flyer is taped to the window: *World-Famous Chicken. See the Dancing Chicken.* In a glass booth right behind the door, there she is.

I put my quarter in the slot. A naked light bulb inside the booth lights up. A plywood turntable on its floor begins to spin. Scratchy polka music comes up from the back. The chicken hops about the spinning floor for a few moments. Then a measured lump of chicken feed comes down the chute at the back of the booth. The chicken eats it. The light goes out.

The Dancing Chicken is a powerful expression of the modern job, and the last word in the miserable false joys of subjugation and confinement. The audience pays, the chicken eats, and, when she's fat, gets eaten. It's a system. It's a business. Another egg is hatched and it goes on.

The cashier takes my dollar bill and gives me dimes for pinball. "Don't feel bad, mister. That chicken booth suck- ered millions of people before you came along."

"I don't want dimes, I want more quarters," I reply.

Lately, the turntable is broken and doesn't spin, but the chicken jumps around exactly as before.

3

The value of the dollar continues to slide. The sweatshops and factories are moving to foreign countries and taking their miserable jobs with them. Regret is replacing the hope of something better. Tourism is the big growth industry. The country is in trouble. Our great city is dying.

When America was doing well, New York City epitomized its glory. Now New York leads the world only in wealth, luxury, dissipation, squalor, dirt, and indifference.

Already, people cannot afford their rent unless they just arrived. The cops are in groups and in cars. Buildings fall down and the homeless move into the ruins. Religions, art movements, and philosophies abound. High culture is sacred. Pornography, prostitution, and drugs are everywhere. And brutality has replaced sentimentality as the culture's pet aesthetic.

Already, the evidence of human occupation has been replaced by tourists, modern architecture, marauding lawless youths, drawn curtains, triple-locked doors, and an obsession with television. On television, they show a world more mean and violent than the reality the viewers cannot afford to go out in.

The rich and respectable classes still claim leadership, but they are afraid of their cleaning ladies and doormen, and exploited by their machines. Their discipline is dissolving as their commitment no longer meets their commitments. They have already tried and failed, and will now give anything and everything to the butler, if only that institution won't desert them. Faced with the breakdown of a civilization organized to serve them, they write letters to the newspapers complaining about graffiti, unruly bicyclists, and loud radios on the street.

The classes that used to work and dream are being laid off, blown out, discharged, and left wandering.

Urban decay is selective; it is not local. There is no more location. Our media, our trade, even our neighbors are global now. But when people believe that their dreams will not come true, they start to live exclusively in the present. And people living in the present do not receive life through an abstracted global view: they notice only the metaphors that disturb the schedule of their carefully sensualized lives.

From the grumpy crowd waiting for the bus, a voice rises: "This place is getting to be just like Babylon. You know, Babylon was a real nice place when they were going good."

The future feels biblical. Nothing can be done about it. Therefore, it has nothing to do with me.

Fifty years ago, people faced with social collapse hit the road because they were ashamed to be seen in failure. Today, there are suburbs where the hobos camped; shame and failure now keep us where we are. Detached from place, we are all runaways from way back, already in hiding.

The realization of modern isolation is itself a barbaric influence. The word is out. We are Babylon.

4

Another pedestrian was killed by a falling roof tile, at the same location as before, so they've decided it's a sniper's work and not pernicious gravity.

The cops closed off a street to evict a tenant who "hasn't paid his rent in years" and was armed with a shotgun. POLICE LINE DO NOT CROSS read the sawhorse, and sprayed across it in red letters, ALL COPS ARE SUBHUMAN GORILLAS.

The Water Department glued a notice to the front door and slipped a copy under it: *Warning. Effective immediately. Do not drink water from the tap until it has been boiled for a minimum of 20 minutes.* The markets all ran specials on bottled drinking water.

A famous European scientist, in town for an international conference, had his briefcase, containing all the raw data on twenty years of research, ripped off by a junkie. Four days later, it turned up soaking wet, in an empty lot on Fifth Street.

A predawn radio jingle ranted, "Food stamps can help you, / Food stamps can help you, / Food stamps can help you / Make ends meet!" A message from the New York State Food Stamp Program that the needy never heard. They were already gathered at the welfare office, waiting for it to open. The old lady across the hall didn't get her food stamps this month. They told her that she was deceased and that her file had been closed.

The Department of Health, right across from the courthouse, held hearings to decide on the closing of public hospitals in the poorest districts. From the windows of the seventh floor, we watched busloads of marching cops with bullhorns and horses deploy, but not a single protestor showed up.

In the suburbs, they are still driving big cars at speeds of maximum fuel consumption. They live in big houses. They are warm in winter. They eat big. And they are again blaming the poor.

In the suburbs, incidents of racially motivated arson, vandalism, and graffiti have tripled in the last year. Fire-bombings, cross burnings, "KKK All the Way," swastikas, and "nigger." Suburban opulence, designed as security, has turned to fear. They can't protect what they've already got; they can't even keep track of it, and all they believe in is more. In Valley Stream, Long Island, after a cross-burning incident, a hundred white families formed an association to keep home listings off the open market and away from blacks.

In the suburbs, the commuters are sharpening the edges of coins to cut the palm of the toll collectors as they cross the bridge to the city. The toll collectors have taken to wearing gloves.

Frightened, thwarted, and bound by the city, the suburbs are secretly hoping that it will die and release them, because they feel as oppressed as everyone else.

The self-destructive urge is everywhere.

5

In this climate, notions of strength revert to the body. Art becomes less manufacture and more personal expression. The desire for fame gives way to the desire for attention; dreaming is replaced by pretending. Festival and ceremony legitimatize their subjects. Where there is no future, you've got to eliminate the middle man and learn to understand retroactively.

At the head of the Halloween parade a police car barked, "Get back, get back on the sidewalk or we'll stop the parade." Same as they had for the Pope, except for the guy grabbing the back bumper dressed in convict stripes and matching pillbox hat, dragging a ball and chain.

Following was a corps of Fu Manchus with black turbans and scarlet robes—on roller skates. They smoked reefer to the conga beat, mostly Latino teenagers, but among them were a few white men with saggy legs and big beer guts. Businessmen and construction workers in another time, but keeping right up, just as graceful and rhythmical, just as swift.

A giant dragon held up by a dozen people with poles

swooped through the crowd and made a four-foot Superman cry. A man in top hat and tails carried the skyline of New York on his shoulders and a theater marquee on his back with his own name up in little lights. A woman with a black rag over her face carried a head in her hand. A lizard crawled the concrete on elbows and knees. A human ham sandwich sported Swiss cheese in great detail.

A troop of victims wrapped in bandages moaned as they marched past. A set of block letters on legs in black tights stumbled, bumping into one another, and whining as they changed places, expressing the pain of literacy in these times.

A trombone section of bearded nuns headed a big band. Their Mother Superior closed his slide and moved through the ranks of ballerinas, butterflies, and pirates. "Jennifer," he shouted to a gossamer-winged fairy, "come up toward the front and be quiet. This is no time to fall apart."

A chicken ten feet high danced. Two boys twirled burning torches in unison. Sword-swallowers and fire-eaters washed it down with beer and pizza.

Monsters and devils frightened strangers, but they liked it. Phony fear to demystify frightening times; exhibitionists and extremists all, safe behind a mask.

The people who normally worked the street were also parading. Beggars, pimps, whores, pickpockets, and general hustlers. Or maybe they were gentlefolk, dressed up as bad. No telling on Halloween. The cold-weather pagan energies of the harvest have re-emerged from a disused holiday once left to children. A sense of ritual that cannot be televised has come back.

No wonder the tourists are flocking here.

6

We used to be the tourists. We used to pick the fashionable spots and overrun them with our wealth and technol-

ogy. We were the ugly Americans who drove the natives
crazy, envious, grateful, and finally to acting inferior. Now
we are the quaint ones who they come to stare at. They get
the taxis on rainy days, and the bargains at the Salvation
Army store. They buy whatever they see, because these
sky-high prices that cripple us are cheap compared to
those where they come from.

Tourists photograph untouchables sleeping in the street
and ask directions of whoever's in the greatest hurry. They
even come to night court, all primped. Jolly scrubbed
faces, overdressed. Oblivious, smiling. Entertained.

For centuries, America received outcasts and refugees
who kissed the earth on the land of wealth and freedom
and embraced its dream. Now they come, and after a few
weeks of the American Way of Life, first class, they go
back through the Golden Door and home. It's an insult to
our Statue of Liberty.

But New York bows and smiles. They've redesigned the
subway map so out-of-towners can read it, and brought
back wholesome souvenirs. They've refurbished the flop-
houses and patched up the monuments. Long on history
and short on cash, New York must sell its charming company like any other fallen glory.

Seats of power are never tourist towns. When tourists
arrive, you know the power has moved to wherever they
came from.

7

Vaughan was demoted. He's scheduled to be a court part
specialist again, soon. They asked him to keep a log on the
rest of us, showing when we were working and when we
were goofing off. He quibbled about the definition of
"goofing" and then refused. They told him it showed he
didn't have the drive necessary to make it in management.

"First they convinced me to stop hustling on the street, get an education, and catch on to their values. Now they tell me I can't get over because I don't have the edge of the street. They said I lacked the killer instinct, as if they ever knew about that." He laughed, but it mattered.

Soon it was a minor detail. His father took ill, diagnosed as terminal cancer, and his girlfriend lost their baby.

Vaughan is ambivalent about his father and feels sorry for his mother, who has to stay home and nurse her husband. He is absolutely devastated by the loss of the child, but he can't let Kitty find out. So his workself goes along, buying Kitty her morning juice and saying mother and child are doing just fine.

He's quieter now and withdrawn. He doesn't speak so much about his dream of helping disturbed youth, and more of his sentences begin with, "If they gave me a job I could believe in . . . If they gave me a house someplace else . . . If they gave me the damn forty acres and a mule . . ."

He screens his sorrow through his job mask. Management is impressed by how seriously he has taken his demotion. His peers are all surprised. Nobody knows what he's going through.

Ever since Charles came back from his honeymoon, he's done nothing but loaf, strut, and reign.

"Here's a man trying to start a family behind this job, and he acts like he doesn't care. What does he think is going to happen?" Vaughan asked.

"Well, he passed the test for the State Police, and you know how much he has his heart set on carrying a gun," I said.

"That isn't solid. They haven't called him. It isn't like Charles," Vaughan said, baffled.

The mystery was solved with Charles's resignation. He's accepted a job from the state of New York as a Minorities

Specialist in Disabilities. He doesn't even know what the title means, and he won't get to carry a gun, but the salary is equal to that of three and a half court part specialists. There is great envy around the office.

Kitty took the same test and was insulted by losing out to a relative fool, but pregnancy has turned her attention to more spiritual matters. Last week she hit a number for $600.

"My father came to me in a dream and asked for the $50 I owe him. I told him I'd pay if he gave me a number. So he gave me 582. I knew it was my number as soon as he said it. Fifty-two is the year I was born. I always play that in combination, I just never knew where to put the last number."

"582 came up last Friday," I said. "That's funny. I got a new phone number last Friday and the exchange is 582."

"What's funny about it?" she said.

"Did you at least give your father his $50 back?"

"I already paid him," she said, "in the dream."

"Kitty, where would I be able to place a bet on a number?"

"Anywhere," she said. "Probably right here."

"No," I said. "Not in the courthouse."

"Well, look how many people you got out here," she said, gesturing across the lobby. "That's more than enough for somebody to keep a book. And if they ain't, you can start keeping your own. But let me find out for you. Ain't no one gonna trust a white man."

In fact, there were two number books being kept, within convenient distance.

8

The Afro-Jewish relationship is logically one of compassion. Historically, both worshipped a God with a clear relationship to His people, who promised to become a practical reality through a terrible deliverance that would sever the guilty past. Both peoples prayed for restoration by removing the sins of their own age and dreamed of a Promised Land. Sharing persecution, they were natural allies, and acted as such for generations in New York City. But at present they just read about each other in the papers, eyeball back and forth on the train, and avoid voluntary contact.

At the courthouse, however, the peoples remain linked. The ghetto myth of the sharp Jewish lawyer persists, and though exceptions abound, generally Jews are judges, lawyers, and bosses; blacks are defendants and workers.

Isolated at the bottom of the system's society, I share the Jewish privilege of the pinnacle and the black resentment of the base. Only my attitude keeps me from being promoted; only my presence keeps me from being disliked. It's a wide tightrope.

I thank God for the few anachronistic gangsters, gamblers, and burglars of the old school who appear as the Jewish defendants, along with the feisty Hasidic sluggers and the drunk, disorderly, and berserk that every tribe produces.

But there aren't many. Little Joe says there were thirty-two Jewish prisoners serving time at Rikers Island when he first went there. Since the release of the last rabbi connected to the big nursing-home scandal, there hasn't been one.

When they chided the judge for suggesting an adjourn date that fell on a Jewish holiday, or when the court stiffened and the cop began to shake because the defense attorney said, "I want the name and shield number of the arresting officer. He made an anti-Semitic remark to me in the halls," I shared the privilege and I felt the draft.

European Jews emigrated to New York with a history of

persecution and suffering. Here they got more of the same at first, and resigned themselves to it. Then, as they prospered and secured their political foothold, Hitler killed 6 million Jews in Europe, and the security achieved here didn't take. But the power reduced both Jewish fear and anti-Semitism to subtle implication, devoid of legitimacy.

At the same time, the persecution and suffering of black America remained, as always, stark and blatant. The Black Experience was a living embodiment of the Jewish Romance, which the Jewish Experience no longer was.

As the Jews moved out of urban poverty to suburban paradise and American identities, the blacks moved in from down South, amazed by their predecessors' complaints and sense of suffering.

The last Jews to leave the ghetto were the landlords and shopkeepers, and consistent with those roles, they left on bad terms, retaining control. And it being America, everyone said the wrong thing and caught the right implication, consistent with institutional racism.

On the job, I politic for my people and try to set an example. When told that Jews give money, I give Charles a generous wedding check. I buy all their Girl Scout cookies and church raffle tickets. I do this for World Jewry.

Do not judge us by what you see here, I plead. In other times and other places, we do much grander things than this. We are not usually guardians and administrators; we are lovers and layabouts, too. We are sign painters and scholars, wrestlers and holy men, roofers and hoofers, high-class tailors and baseball players. For eight hundred years we grew potatoes in Eastern Europe and were beaten up regularly. We are not used to business, power, and wealth. This New York experience has warped us. Spiritually, this is our worst, and in no way typical of our history.

And then the story broke about a secret nuclear bomb

test, exploded jointly by Israel and the Union of South Africa. This was worse than when they embraced Nixon. A newspaper was waved in my face, an explanation demanded.

What could I say? What could I feel was the value of the suffering for centuries that was ours?

9

"I never will forget that Dante's *Inferno*," said Vaughan. "Worst damn book I ever read."

"Don't say that," I said.

"Did they make you read it, too?"

"They make everybody read it. When a book has been around that long and impressed that many people, it's part of the heritage—part of explaining how we got to be the way we are. It's too late to read it because you like it or you don't. But aren't you curious just to see what has held up for five hundred years?"

"Held up for who?" said Vaughan. "We were over in Africa minding our own business. Never even heard of Dante's *Inferno*. For us, it's just a trick to make sure we feel inferior."

"Yes, but as long as they have the power, their knowledge is the only knowledge. And if you don't own it, the best you can do is to learn it."

"That's the Jewish method," said Vaughan. "I'll just never be that well-trained a nigger. This little PROMIS training is about as much as I can take."

10

Judge Woof is no longer running his court with the same enthusiasm and good cheer. In his back, a sciatic nerve is being pinched by a ruptured spinal disc. The pain pulls at his face and his patience, and makes him seem as weary and overwhelmed as the others.

Little Joe, feeling sorry for a thief, stood up for him in night court and got him paroled into his custody. As soon as they got to his apartment in Brooklyn, the thief stole $300 and left. It didn't make Joe angry, but the release of the last Jewish prisoner did.

"He's out, you know," Joe said. "He stole all that money, and on one year, he served nine and a half months. Three months off for good behavior, less two weeks for the chicken sandwich he was caught with."

"I remember it," I said.

"He's a terrible man. The first time I saw him, I walked right up to him and called him a shame on the Jews. But he's an old man, and Corrections felt sorry for him. They let him do all his time in the infirmary. I felt sorry for him, too. I used to bring him kosher food. His wife prepared it for me, and Corrections looked the other way. It wasn't allowed, you know. They took a chance. I took a chance. And after all that, you know what he's doing now?"

"No."

"On the day he got out, he filed suit against the Department of Corrections for not giving him a big enough space to pray in. The ingrate. I'd like to box his ears."

Big Jim is so under control you hardly know he's in charge. He orders his court officers around in whispers, and even when he screams at the court reporter for ignoring his orders to put away all newspapers, you can hardly hear what he's saying. All I know is that he comes to work on a big chrome motorcycle, and he tried to sell me his portable electric typewriter because his girlfriend just got a new one.

I pegged him for a poet, but he just shook his head and whispered, "You can't play head games with Einstein."

He drives a taxi at night.

Mr. Slice is more accessible. He's past his provisional period and now has his gun. He is down at the shooting range every chance he gets, and is dressing in white turtleneck sweaters, worn underneath a big shoulder holster. They call him John Shaft, Private Investigator, which he likes, but he will never be a real firearms fanatic.

"Last night, after dinner, I was sitting in the kitchen, oiling the holster and playing with it, you know," Mr. Slice said unself-consciously. "I got the hammer cocked, and I couldn't get the damn thing back down. I had to go around to an abandoned building and fire it off before I could put it away. Scared the shit out of me. I could have been arrested."

Officer Lockheed, pining away, has turned from recreation to devotion in his quest for baseball. "I got to get my swing back. I got to get in shape, man. I know I can hit big-league pitching. I could always hit good, but I got to get out there and play. You see how all the big names are coming from down South and California. They can play all year. How am I supposed to get in shape in this weather? I got to find a gym or something, because this is serious. They're signing these guys up for millions of dollars. I want to play for the Pittsburgh Pirates. It's my only chance."

The court reporter takes down the record in his wrinkled raincoat and college boy's khaki hat, which he forgets to remove. He shivers in the overheated courtroom, even so. And he is so broke that he's picking up newspapers from the audience. He still buys his own candy, though. When the lawyers pause, he pours Cracker Jacks into his mouth from the box, and shakes his head as he chews, like a cat. Everyone notices.

"You keep eating when all day long I tell you not to," shouted the judge. "Look at yourself, Mr. Taylor. Lift up your head and take control of yourself. Take off your hat, and save your appetite for a good dinner in Chinatown."

"I tried that years ago," the court reporter said.

"Well," said the judge, "wasn't that better?"

"No," said the court reporter. "It got me so I couldn't eat at all. I still can't eat at a table. I can't even go into a restaurant. I got to be doing something or going somewhere to be hungry. I can't stand to sit and just eat."

11

When life in a society no longer fulfills its expectations, its members turn to chance. To win at gambling is to be chosen by God. And the payoff is immediate; all other forms of raising capital require a future.

But for two days no numbers were accepted for play in New York City. All the rackets runners and bankers were in Albany demonstrating at the State Capitol against the government competing for their business.

"The numbers is the dominant financial institution where we live," said Kitty. "That's where you cash a check, take a loan, get advice—just like a bank for you people. And besides, they're willing to pay $2 million a year in taxes if they're legal, and that's a lot more than the state expects to get for its numbers game."

"And it tells you how much they're already paying out," Vaughan added.

"I see you playing pretty regular now, how you doing?" asked Kitty.

"No luck," I said. "I got myself a dream book and everything, but . . . I guess it just takes time."

"White people can't dream numbers," she said. "Everybody knows that."

"That's a pretty prejudiced thing to say," I said. "Especially after all the cultural crossovers that this society has been through."

"Don't go getting on me," she said. "Any pink fool believe that, he can lose his money any way he wants."

All other fiduciary institutions take money and talent out of the ghetto. We put it back, said the placard. The charm and paraphernalia of play make the player forget that the urge to gamble grows out of a sense of loss. Waiting for divine intervention is a passive act that comes after the belief in making your own way has gone.

12

The plumbers are fixing the sink in the pens. They forgot their I.D. badges and many important pipes and wrenches. They amble back and forth, right through the proceedings, smoking cigarettes and wearing hats. They leave the velvet rope unhooked and drop pieces of wax paper with dripping pickles on the floor. "Let's see some I.D.!" "Hey, you, no smoking!" "Hats off!" "Hey. Hey! Don't do that!" the uniformed court officers shout, but the plumbers carry their workplace with them and can't even hear it.

LAS: How do you feel, sir?

D: I feel fine.

LAS: That's a bad sign, sir. You're in court, accused of a crime. You are not supposed to feel fine.

D: What difference does it make, I'm guilty.

LAS: Your honor, I think we have a disposition.

DA: Please state your name.

D: Sweeper, Sheldon Sweeper.

DA: Is that your lawyer standing next to you? Did you confer with him about this case before entering a plea?

D: Yes. Yes.

DA: And on the afternoon of January 31, in Union Square Park, did you willfully appropriate property belonging to one—

BENCH: Did you take the wallet?

D (*laughing*): Yes.

BENCH: Sir, why are you laughing?

D: Because the wallet had one dollar in it and I took it from my wife.

BENCH: Is a psychiatric examination in order here?

LAS: No, sir. Those are the alleged facts.

BENCH: Then let's not waste time. You took the wallet, right?

D: Yes.

BENCH: Conditional discharge. Next.

LAS: They're offering you six days if you will plead to a petit larceny.

D: Six days. They must be crazy.

LAS: No. Let me explain. You get two days' credit for good behavior, two days' credit for time served, and since there's no more weekend release, they'll let you out this afternoon. If you don't plead, they want to set bail and you might be in jail for some time. Three days at least.

D: I guess I'll take it.

BENCH: Okay, Mr. DA. Stick to the facts and keep it brief.

DA: State your name.

D: Billy Do Wops.

DA: Did you take the pot of flowers?

D: No. I took one flower from the front of the store. I didn't even go inside. Just one flower, wrapped in plastic.

DA: The plea is acceptable to the People.

BENCH: The plea is acceptable to the court.

VOICE OF THE DEPARTMENT OF CORRECTIONS (*from the pens*): Whichever one of you lawyers is known as Cunt, your client is asking for you, in the back.

VOICE OF YOUTH (*from the pens*): Get this fucking faggot out my face. I want a Jew lawyer!

AGED VOICE (*singing, from the pens*): "How much is that doggie in the window, the one with the waggily tail—arf,

arf. How much is that doggie in the window—bow-wow. I do hope that doggie's for sale."

COURT REPORTER: Hold it. I can't hear a goddamn thing. You'll have to get some quiet back there before I can take any more.

BRIDGEMAN: Sorry about that, man. There's nothing I can do. That is the sound of reality back there. If you lived in their neighborhoods, lived that life, you'd holler too when you got locked up.

AGED VOICE (*singing, from the pens*): "Roll out the barrel, we'll have a barrel of fun. Roll out—"

The dull crack of a punching fist interrupts. Silence follows.

BRIDGEMAN: Gratch, grand larceny. Bring him right up.

ARREST REPORT: Peculiarities, deformities, scars, and tattoos: Doesn't bathe.

PRIOR RECORD: 1955, Palm Beach, Florida, breaking and entering. 1966, New York, grand larceny. No disposition reported. And yesterday, caught in the act of removing the radio from a police car.

CURRENT ADDRESS: Zip Code 10040 (any street).

Frank Gratch, aka Frankie Grace, aka Johnny Rae, aka Frank Sinatra. White male, age fifty-two. Small, thin, with a week's growth of white beard and softly humming "It's Magic" while his puffed eye turns black-and-blue.

D: You remember me, don't you? I played the lead part in *Pinocchio*, in 1945. The Lincoln High School production. John Garfield came to see it. You remember 1945, don't you? It was the year Joe DiMaggio hit forty-nine home runs.

BENCH: In 1945, Joe DiMaggio was in the Army. Now, be quiet, sir. Rely on your lawyer to address the court.

A/O: Your honor, I've had two days of this. Guy's driving me crazy.

BENCH: Does he have anywhere to go?

A/O: He told me he was sharing a penthouse with Liza Minnelli at the Carlyle Hotel.

LAS: Did he make any other statements? I assume you're serving Statement Notice.

DA: Yes. The defendant stated: I was going to give it back. I just wanted to listen to WKTU. I love the disco sound.

BENCH: Better come up, Counselors.

COURT REPORTER: The disco sound. I love it, too.

The lawyers confer. The court reporter puts it down for a psychiatric examination.

BRIDGEMAN: Psst. Hey, mister, I bet you don't know "America the Beautiful."

D: I know it, I know it good, but . . .

BRIDGEMAN: You're just saying that, you don't really know it.

D: I do so.

BRIDGEMAN: You do not. Now, stand up straight, keep your hands at your sides, and be quiet.

D: "Oh beautiful, for spacious skies, for amber waves of grain-n-n. For purp—"

The defendant exits on the thrust of four tacklers.

LAS: Waive the production of my client.

The defendant is barefoot. On his head he wears a sheet of aluminum foil, molded into a Davy Crockett hat, complete with tail. On his face, he wears a slice of white bread from the bologna sandwich they gave him in the pens, glued to it with mustard, with eyeholes torn out. He enters, pulling his sneakers on a leash made out of their laces. A trickle of urine runs down his leg. He wears no pants.

D: C'mon, Rover. C'mon, boy.

BENCH: That's enough.

D: I want to thank you all for coming.

BENCH: Get him out.

———

The defendant is a career criminal. Thirty prior arrests, six years of state time. He is holding a red straw hat over his crotch.

LAS: Your honor, this was a mild altercation in the toilets of the bus station.

A/O: Yeah, but it took four officers to cuff him.

LAS: May we approach?

BENCH: Yes.

BRIDGEMAN: All right, mister, you're pitching for Baltimore and I come up for the Pirates. Last game of the World Series. The bases are loaded, now what are you going to throw me?

D: Leave me alone, man.

BRIDGEMAN: Curve ball. You thought I was a sucker for a curve, but I don't swing. Ball one. Now what you throw?

D: I can't hear what they're saying.

BRIDGEMAN: All right, hands at your sides.

D: I can't.

BRIDGEMAN: You heard me. Put the hat on the table and your hands at your side.

D: Look, I'm losing my pants, here. If I take away the hat, like this— I'll show you.

BRIDGEMAN: Okay, okay. I don't need to see it. Just keep it covered with the hat. Okay?

LAS: At this time my client pleads guilty to being disorderly, waives formal arraignment, waives any adjournment for sentencing, and stands ready.

BENCH: Time served. Get him a pair of pants and send him home.

BENCH: What happened? This arrest is three days old. Where is the other defendant?

A/O: It's all the same dude, sir. I locked him up for gambling. Robbery, sexual abuse, and sodomy took place in the police van on the way to court.

BENCH: How could that happen?

DA: According to my write-up, your honor, he was hand-cuffed and sitting next to a foreign student from Iran. Somehow he managed to pass the student's wallet and glasses around the van and rub his cock in the student's face. Money and property belonging to the student were recovered.

BENCH: And what was the student charged with?

A/O: 511 of the VTL. He ignored too many parking tickets for too long. I think there was twenty-nine suspensions.

BENCH: Oh, my God, what happened to the poor fellow?

A/O: He was ordered to pay up the tickets.

DA: We're asking $10,000 bail because Officer Acevedo was bit in the leg, Officer Baldonado was hit in the head with his own club, and Officer Kelly was scratched on the neck.

LAS: My client wishes to inform the court that he bit the officer only because he was down on the floor with three cops beating him and had only his teeth to defend himself.

UCO: Excuse me, your honor, there's a man in the audience who wants to speak with you. He says his name is Big Red. Do you know him?

BENCH: Well, I can see that you don't play the numbers, child. Big Red is the most famous tip sheet in the whole of uptown.

UCO: What should I tell him?

BENCH: I'd be surprised if he really is Big Red, but you tell him to wait until his name is called, just like everybody else. And if he leaves before, a warrant will be issued for his arrest.

BENCH: He stole a bottle of hot sauce because his wife was cooking meat loaf? Is that the allegation?

A/O: And after the arrest, she realized that she had some.

Deponent is informed that defendant did promote and participate in a dog fight by pushing dogs into each other, pouring wine on their cuts, and taking bets ... Deponent is informed by Manhattan Court employee that defendant, acting in concert with another, did borrow a pencil from informant and add fines paid to three of the dockets listed ... did take a box containing parochial-school uniforms for young girls, without permission or authority ... found with a sledgehammer in his hand, pushing a sink and toilet on a stolen hand truck, defendant did lower said plumbing articles from a floor of said building without permission or ... did threaten the chef with a hunting knife to make sure that he cooked the steak rare, and passed out before he could be fingerprinted (methadone addict) ... did sneak into the circus and come up in a cage full of bears ... did wrap her newborn baby in two sheets and a pillow case belonging to the hospital and remove them without permission or authority ...

LAS: Your honor, I want to apologize for my outbursts. I've just come back from vacation and I'm not used to this atmosphere yet. I hope I haven't offended you in any way.
BENCH: Counselor, you were the only interesting thing that happened all day.
COURT REPORTER: What do you expect? A poor man is going to jail, that's all that happens here. What could be interesting about that?
BENCH: Poor person, you mean. But what can I do about it?
DA: These guys must be kidding. This place is nothing. They should go out in the suburbs where these people are just starting to cross the borders. They have two guards on

the rail, each with a shotgun. The defendants are brought in handcuffed and only unlocked when their case is called. They aren't allowed to plead at arraignment. After the case is heard, they put the cuffs back on. They snap 'em so it tears the skin, and then they take them in the back and beat them. I used to work out there. It's almost vigilantes.

CHAPTER NINE

1

The blackened snow is receding from the garbage heaps. The city's trees, deformed by their search for light in a landscape of ever deepening canyons, are twisting and budding. Bats, bears, and dormice have awakened from their winter sleep, and people are back on the street, hustling each other and sowing the jive of next year's mayhem.

Winter thaws, the cycle turns, and court is filling up.

A bird flew into AT-1. It didn't interrupt the flow, but every eye in the room went to it. As it slapped and bumped along the edge of the ceiling, a murmur arose.

BRIDGEMAN: Quiet in here. Let's have some quiet. And somebody get rid of the bird.

A/O: When it shits on the judge's head, we'll have to shoot it.

BRIDGEMAN: Hey, your honor, watch out for the birdie.

BENCH: I don't have to, everybody else is. May we proceed?

The bird discovered a clean patch of window, but couldn't understand the glass, which it crashed into, head first. Stunned, it fell through the blinds to the windowsill, raised itself up, and tried again. It was awful, but the architect had put the windows up high, to make them escape-proof. Down on the floor, we watched helplessly.

The engineer was called in. He tried to open the window, but it wouldn't budge. A brave court officer put a chair on the prisoner's bench and climbed high enough to place a torn-down paper cup filled with water. The bird drank from it.

All afternoon, the determined bird banged its head on the window pausing longer between attempts. Midway through night court, it found a resting place. In the morning, there were feathers on the windowsill and blood on the blinds. The water was changed, and a cup of birdseed, brought from home by Big Jim, was placed beside it. As the bird ate, the crew, led by their captain, delicately carried the water and seed out of the courtroom, and the bird followed, all the way to the park.

2

In the civil service, life grows easy and linear. It has taken years to realize that this is the new bureaucracy, a new generation, predominantly young, black, and successful, and therefore proving a lot looser than the best behavior everyone began with.

They wear their own clothes now, or are used to the styles they thought were expected of them. Gay men now wear earrings and handkerchiefs; married women slop around in fuzzy slippers. The old ladies have chipped in and bought a refrigerator, and are thinking about a stove. Tap and Latin dance lessons are available during the lunch hour. And the afternoon of payday has declined into a bazaar.

Management is in a tizzy. Cooking and eating are not allowed; they bring mice into the office. Trading during working hours is forbidden. Everything but work, during working hours, is forbidden. How does it look?

But the advantages of getting over, en masse, are irresistible. They have capital and a market now, and to one another they sell peanut brittle, cookies, boxed chocolates, soap, jogging suits, raffle tickets, undergarments, chain letters, jewelry, astrological explanations, religious objects, life insurance, and jeans. All delivered on payday.

It's an outrage, but management is civil service, too, and learning what it's like to live in this new bureaucracy.

So far, two marriages in the big room on the seventh floor, and many hot romances, both real and for show. One of the real ones broke off after she bought him a motorbike and lunch every other day, on the understanding he would lead her to the altar. When he said they were through, she pulled out a knife, leaned across the blotter, and stabbed him in the stomach. Next morning, she was arraigned in AT-1. Everybody came down to watch.

3

When the ever-present smell of fear passes for no smell, the fetor of the city takes on a slight perfume. Decay is a transformation—an arc in a cycle, not its end. As institutions crumble in doubt and disbelief, some institutional other thing is busy being born.

Life in social decline turns from the future to the present, from ideas to pleasures, and from abstraction to sensuality. As civilization ebbs, the human spirit flows. The feared collapse is also a return to a slower, simplified life.

After all, if not for the dangerous high-crime areas, none of us could afford to live in New York. Reclaimed and added to the "revitalized urban core," such true communities are broken and scattered in the hills of New Jersey, replaced by the telephones and credit cards of faceless money.

We live in a time when it is easy to recognize the counterfeits of the past, under assumed names, calling themselves the future. We know who owns which metaphors, even if none of them works anymore.

The coming of spring is a call to action—time to plant, time for greed and ambition to consider its expectations for the harvest. And nobody wants to think that far ahead.

When we were fat, we tried to make life perfect, and failed. Now we are lean. The time to fix what's wrong has passed. No more illusions.

4

Of all the perfected forms of judicial administration, the highest is reserved for prostitutes. Gamblers, jewel thieves, drug dealers, and gypsy fortune-tellers are all equally professional, but they don't get the exposure. One-third of all arrests in the jurisdiction are for prostitution—over 30,000 cases a year. It's part of the tourist business, part of show business, and part of the decline.

Modern crime is largely amateur, spontaneous, and random. The system has no influence on it, deterrent or otherwise. But prostitutes respond to the system and give pleasure to it.

They support their lawyers, and give the cops tender

young bodies for easy collars and a well of available over-time. In return, the lawyers spring them quickly, and the cops answer their calls, protect them, and save their lives.

In court, prostitutes exercise their constitutional rights, voluntarily enter a plea of guilty, are sentenced, pay their fines, and step out in the shortest possible time. Veteran whores, given the right judge and bridgeman, can plead out at a rate of twelve per minute. The legislature can do nothing about a mediocre judge in night court, but the prostitutes can turn him into a genius who disposes of 180 cases in a single session.

Prostitutes can afford their fines and don't consume expensive jail space. Their numbers swell the arrest totals, and prove the rising rate of crime that must be met with appropriations. And their cases are not trying. Over-searched souls need not be plumbed to judge them. Going through the system is just part of their job, too. They don't provoke the anxiety of blind judgment. And being prostitutes, they show a lot of flesh and say outrageous things, and in other ways bring color to the ashen cheeks of advocates.

Prostitution is a tragedy of our new order. Both the coldhearted shame that buys its shot of life, and the pool of aimless, disturbed children who wind up selling it, are sad and sorry ends. But it's as ancient a profession as the law, and where would the system be without it?

5

BRIDGEMAN: Docket Number Y009999, Cherry Blossom, prostitution on the complaint of Officer Dailey. Companion matter, Docket Number Y010000, Blossom Cherise, prostitution, on the complaint of Officer Nightly. Step up, please.

BENCH: How can I fine you? You have 103 previous arrests and two outstanding warrants.

D: Then I ain't gonna plead until my lawyer gets here. This here Legal Aid had garlic pizza for lunch.

BENCH: The offer is five days, young lady; take it or leave it.

D: Fuck you.

BENCH: Motion denied, let's set a date.

The defendant put the complainant on the street, as a prostitute, three year ago. Last February, they were married and he stabbed her. She was in the hospital for two days. Night before last, he cut a necklace into the base of her neck with a razor blade.

In court, she pulls down her polo-neck sweater and shows her scabs to the judge. But she won't say he did it.

The case is tossed. He is offered 90 days on his warrant and takes it. As they lead him away, she weeps, slips him a $50 bill and a carton of cigarettes, and tells him she loves him.

The defendant is dressed in patent-leather pumps, fishnet stockings, and an iridescent leotard. Around her hips is a gold belt. The weather is not as warm as it was last night.

BENCH: What did you do, bust Radio City?

A/O: What do you mean?

BENCH: Looks like you've got one of the Rockettes there.

D: Richie . . .

A/O looks away and shakes his finger no.

D: Richie, why you don't ax me for pussy? I'll give it to you free, if you don't bust me.

A/O: Shh . . . later.

D: You going uptown after this, Richie?

A/O: Yeah.

D: Well, wait for me. I'll meet you right outside.

———

BRIDGEMAN: Docket Number Y999728, Precious Womble. Pros, petit larceny, and possession of stolen property in the third degree.

DA: What happened, Officer?

A/O: Regular pros-john ripoff. She took his wallet.

DA: Observe anything?

A/O: No. I collared her when she came back for her teeth.

DA: Her teeth?

A/O: She took them out to give him a blow-job and left them in his car.

PA: My client says she'll take the offer if the arresting officer will buy her a pack of cigarettes.

A/O: No. Absolutely not.

D: Aw, Tony. All the overtime you earn off me and you won't fetch me a lousy pack of cigarettes.

A/O: Yeah, you're getting me a divorce, you're giving me so much overtime.

D (*crying*): I'm sorry. I know I'm a real baby at this, but I'm getting better, you should have seen me a couple of years ago.

UCO: Hey, what are you anyway, a man or a woman?

D: Ain't you man enough to find out for yourself, sucker?

UCO: Well, that's against department regulations. Besides, the way they do these sex operations now, you can't tell by looking.

UCO: All right, on the bench, relax. And if you ain't got no underpants, keep your knees together. Act good now, and maybe I'll take you out to a disco later.

D: Why wait, honey? Let's go now. I want you so bad I'm gonna fuck your brains out.

UCO: Yeah, but will you love me?

D: You get me out of here and I'll show you how much.

UCO: You see, you don't care about my personality. You're treating me like some kind of sex object. What kind of a relationship is that?

LAS: Your honor, my client is not a prostitute. She was out with her husband shopping for a pair of shoes to wear for jury duty, which she begins tomorrow. She is thirty-four years old, the mother of two children, and has no previous record. At 5 foot 3, 165 pounds—well, the court can see from her appearance and demeanor that she is not a prostitute. She was hailing a taxi, not soliciting. . . . Now, don't cry, Mrs. Resurreccio, everything's going to be all right. We'll sue the city and get you $10,000 for this.

6

Over at the prisoner's bench, a prostitute named Lance sits. The computer couldn't handle his sex change, so he's awaiting reprinting; about to burst, he tries to practice patience. At the clerk's desk, a bored court part specialist sits. Nothing is ready, so he's awaiting the passage of time; quietly, he tries to let Big Jim educate him.

"It's just a matter of attitude," says Big Jim. "You've got to understand that this is the best-quality arraignment part in the country. Probably the best in the world. I've been to courtrooms all over the United States. I spent a couple years hanging around the Chicago courts, and then all those years in Brooklyn. Believe me, nothing even approaches the quality of AT-1. You just don't appreciate it."

"Are you serious?" The court part specialist laughs. "How could any court be worse than this?"

"Well, like in Chicago, they don't even call you mister."

Conversation dies as everyone turns to the commotion on the prisoner's bench.

Lance is a big fat black lady with fluorescent orange

earrings, a purple plunging neckline, and a short orange wraparound skirt. Her strawberry-blond hair is messed up. Her behind is huge, her breasts are enormous, and she is not shy or patient.

She crosses and uncrosses her legs nervously, showing lots of juicy thigh. Her bosom heaves and rolls with every move and gesture. It is the size and shape of bosom that cops, lawyers, judges, and portions of the audience share in their dreams.

Lance loves attention. That's why she is always getting into trouble. With a show-business sigh, she blows kisses to the audience, and pulls the drawstring at her neckline. It drops, and out they fall.

A collective gasp implodes. There they are, puffed up by science and plastic to pure photogenia. The proceedings stop. Transfix. Freeze.

Officer Lockheed, weak at the knees himself, reins in the racing minds with the thump of his blackjack against the low wood wall. "All right, mister! Cover 'em up."

Which in Chicago, you see, you wouldn't hear.

7

The worst of our wisdom is the Juveniles. We've had them in AT-1 ever since the legislature moved the adult responsibility for certain violent felonies down to the age of thirteen, where it was fifty years ago, when enlightenment raised it.

Their cases come in special orange jackets and embarrass everyone. Nobody knows the procedures, and the defendants seem unusually small for their age. Alleged monsters of the glee-club and church-choir stereotype.

The birth dates of the juveniles coincide with the era of the great civil rights movement. These are the kids that the dream was for.

But this tiny cherub shot the supermarket manager, dropped the money, and was tackled by a passerby. And this Little Leaguer's pistol was so old and worn that it took three shots before it fired and blew some white boy's head off at point-blank range. And that pink-cheeked eighth-grader "held complainant at knife point and forced him to give oral sex." Complainant is eleven years old. Three other kids from the neighborhood have complained of the same thing.

"Pretty lusty little boy you've got there, Officer," says the assistant DA; he doesn't know what to say. When a social order fears its own children, nobody knows what to say.

8

The arresting officer is 6 foot 8 and hefty. The defendant is 4 foot 4 and slight. They had to wake him up when the case was called and everyone laughed.

BRIDGEMAN: Tough collar, huh?

DA: Is he a bad kid, Officer?

A/O: This kid didn't know his own birthday. I went and saw the mother. She has twelve other kids and didn't remember it. He's never had a birthday party, never got any presents or anything. He's never been treated like he's somebody special, even for one day. I had to stop off and buy him a banana split on the way down here, but I . . . I don't know what to do for him. Sure, he's a bad kid. This is his third felony arrest, and I'm not sure he's thirteen yet.

DA: What did he do?

A/O: Robbed a grocery store and beat up the owner with a baseball bat.

DA: Anybody hurt?

A/O: Fractured skull. And then he set a fire at Central Booking during the strip search.

The charge is prostitution. The rap sheet says eighteen priors, but the officer is sure of at least thirty more. The defendant is in French clothes and false eyelashes, looking like a model on the cover of a magazine. Except the freshness she exudes never makes it all the way from arrest to arraignment. And her mother is in court.

BENCH: If the defendant is only thirteen years old, this case must be transferred to Family Court.

A/O: I spent all day in Family Court. They sent me back here, which is where I started. All I want to do is go home and get some sleep.

BENCH: I'm sorry. We have no jurisdiction.

LAS: Her mother is here, your honor. Couldn't you parole her into her mother's custody and settle it on a return date?

BENCH: That's an idea. Ma'am, do you think you can keep your daughter out of trouble and bring her to Family Court if I send her home with you?

MOTHER: No. I tried before, but she runs off every time. I don't know what goes on inside her.

BENCH: We'll have to remand her.

LAS: Where? Corrections can't accept her until she's been arraigned.

BENCH: Hmmm . . . we do have a problem.

MOTHER: Why don't you just fine her? She can pay.

BENCH: No, ma'am. We can't do anything. It's not within our jurisdiction.

MOTHER: But you already done fined her twenty-five times before.

BENCH: That was before we knew her age. Now that we know it, it's out of our hands.

MOTHER: It is?

A/O: What are we going to do?

BENCH: Second call to see if Corrections will produce her in Family Court in the morning. Next.

*Arrested for assault and possession of a weapon at the
age of ten; arrested twice, for burglary and arson, at
the age of eleven; arrested six times at the age of twelve:
burglary, assault, robbery, burglary, possession of a
weapon (gun), assault; picked up by the police in a coma
from an overdose of pills at the age of thirteen; threw rocks
at a police officer and was identified but not apprehended
at the age of fourteen; and now, at fifteen, the charge is
murder.*

DA: This is a strong case, your honor. It has already been
presented to the grand jury, and we are asking for bail in
the amount of $75,000, despite the defendant's age, as this
is a particularly vicious murder.

LAS: But, your honor, as soon as my client arrived at his
grandmother's house and heard they were looking for him,
he turned himself in. His uncle arranged his coming in.
The uncle is in court and so is his mother. She works as a
domestic and has three other children to support. She informs me that she does have a few hundred dollars' savings, and she is willing to put them up, but nothing like
$75,000.

BENCH: Bail is set in the amount of $25,000, cash or bond.

LAS: $25,000? This isn't a real homicide, your honor. It was
a fight between two armed men.

BENCH: Counselor, the deceased was found stabbed in the
heart with his own knife still in its sheath. What do you
expect me to do?

9

Poachers dwell in the forest, smugglers cling to mountain-
sides and seashores, and maniacs inhabit the city. Forest,
mountain, and sea render humanity savage and fierce; the
city makes them self-destructive and homicidal.

At a certain depth, impenetrable to the soul, the monsters become possible. By pain and failure they are made; by want they are guided to care for nothing but glut. From suffering they pass to crime.

Yet several thousand people live on an average high-crime block of New York. And on average, all but half a dozen of them are ordinary decent people who happen to be poor. The half dozen terrorize the block and all who pass.

The studies—the science and the statistics—will explain the criminal roots of the six, ignoring the thousands. Or vice versa; nobody really knows anything about how social beings are formed, or why.

10

Charles's last day was the Friday of an off week. No paycheck and a freak snowstorm. Nobody was in the mood for anything but getting home, but we had all been invited for a farewell drink.

There was some confusion as to which bar, and we were soaked as we walked from one to the other. "I ain't got no money, but I guess I can steal a little bit from my bills," Kitty said.

"You steal from the bills, they gonna shanghai you, girl," her friend said.

"Oh, they already came for me, and my mother told them I was 5 foot 10 and had three arms and two foreheads, so they out looking for this big black thing, not me."

In the bar, Charles was already downing shots and flitting among the groups he'd invited, rather like at the wedding. While he was gone from our table, his fortune dominated the talk. "He ain't qualified to be no damn disabilities specialist ... $25,000? ... and oh, Lord, why not me."

Some stranger from data entry had been named to succeed Vaughan as supervisor, and Kitty held him responsible. "I bust my ass for you and it don't mean a thing. How you expect me to live on this little salary with a baby coming and everything?"

"You always say I make up stuff, so I'm not saying anything," said Vaughan.

"Quit it, Kitty," I interrupted. "You know Vaughan's getting dumped. He doesn't have anything to say. And you know, deep down, you really care for him."

She grunted.

"C'mon, Kitty. In front of everybody, admit it."

"Well, sometimes I might die for him, and sometimes I want to kill him. And that's the honest truth."

"Brooklyn, you all right," said Charles, toasting Vaughan. "Anyone from Harlem can get over on Brooklyn, and I sure got over on you." We all sipped.

"Kitty, you making a fine baby."

"And, homeboy, I don't even hate white people anymore. Not like I used to."

We sipped again.

"Sorry to be leaving you all," Charles shouted, "but I'm going somewhere."

"You don't have to shout," said Kitty. "Don't you know that since we've been calling ourselves black, we're not so loud anymore. You sound like some old Negro."

Charles looked puzzled and went off to dance. We finished our drinks quietly and left, one at a time. Vaughan and I were the last to go. We sought out Charles to say goodbye, but he insisted we go into the men's room for a private conference.

The place was crowded with young men, relaxing in a manner well within the accepted norms of the community in which they are known. Being of that same community, we faded right in.

"If I was you, Charles, I wouldn't be here," said

Vaughan. "I'd be down with some medical dictionary or something, learning as much as I could about disability. At least how to spell the words. You got a lot going on this thing, Charles."

"Look here, man," said Charles. "Money and violence, that's what I am. That's all I believe." And he smashed his fist into the tile work.

"A disabilities specialist is way beyond violence," I said.

"Yeah," he said, "but I still respect it. And you know, you got to reach back into that bag every once in a while."

"Or at least talk about it," said Vaughan.

Charles laughed, and we all breathed.

"Now, I'm going to tell you something, freedom fighter," he said. "And maybe someday, when the revolution comes, you can save yourself with it. Use it to escape.

"You see, when white people gets drunk, they lie. And when black people gets drunk, they tell the truth."

"Whose truth?" asked Vaughan.

"You see what I'm saying," said Charles. "You get white people drunk, they say, 'You okay.' But drunk niggers say, 'Man, you ain't worth shit.'"

"I see," I said. "Thanks a lot."

"You better remember all this stuff in case you ever write a book," said Charles. "You just put down everything I told you about Harlem. Mix 'em up with sex and kung fu and you got a million-dollar movie right there. You can still do it. You just remember to put in Charles Taliaferro. You hear—T-A-L-I-A-F-E-R-R-O. And you don't say nothing about no chiba."

And that was the last of Charles.

Kitty, who had already arranged an extended pregnancy leave, and who hit another number (285), took one look at Vaughan's successor and left two months early.

Mercifully, Vaughan's father died after only weeks of

suffering. What with the Easter rush, he had to wait five days to get booked into a funeral home. The family came up from Virginia. Vaughan hadn't seen them since his childhood, since his grandmother's funeral, in fact. They are all doing well. Homeowners, and one uncle even has a business, dry cleaning and alterations. To his surprise, Vaughan liked them.

The loss of his father touched Vaughan more deeply than he expected. Almost against his principles, he forgave the old man everything. "Even if he wasn't around when he should have been, he did the best he could, I guess," Vaughan said. But still mourning the loss of his unborn child, he didn't have sufficient grief left over.

Vaughan's winter cold hangs on, keeping his eyes glassy, his nose running, and his pockets filled with balls of rolled-up tissue. The illness suits his mood.

Polite attempts to communicate my concern are thwarted with stern defeatism like, "Every man needs his recreation." I don't like to pry, but I know what his pride means to him. We let it go unspoken.

"We had a meeting at the projects," Vaughan said. "Sort of a reunion. We just sat around talking, finding out what happened to everybody. There was probably five hundred kids there when I was coming up. Every one of us dreamed of getting over, thought we would. And nobody did, except three schoolteachers, one certified public accountant, and me, doing this damn job.

"All the rest are still on the street, so I'm supposed to be satisfied with this. What's the use? We can't make it here. I'm going to wind up right where I started. Maybe that's who I am, anyway. I don't know anymore. Maybe I have to go away to be something better, so I can come back and do some good. Or maybe I'm no better than the rest of them, moving out on my people so I can live white. I am not materialistic, but I have children to look after. They aren't going to make it either, if I stay. And I ain't doing nothing here."

The only smile I've seen on Vaughan lately was on his son Darneer's eighth birthday. He brought him into court and played the big-shot pop. The boy was unimpressed by the proceedings and the privileges granted him. He refused an invitation to sit with the judge and only wanted to go behind the door to the pens, where all the black men went. Neither the District Attorney nor his employees are allowed in the pens. Then he nearly broke into tears at the idea of a good meal and insisted on going to McDonald's.

Spring training came and went for Officer Lockheed. His wife brought the twins home, but after four days of quarreling took them back to her mother's. Lockheed wanted to shoot someone. He even started reading magazines for mercenary soldiers. "I'll shoot anybody for money," he said. "I don't care whose side they're on."

After that, he decided that he should become a lawyer and traded in his imaginary baseball bat for an imaginary bath towel. "Got to be a lawyer if I'm going to come out of the swimming pool behind my mansion on a hot summer day," he said, going through the motions of drying his back with it.

"In the Marines, we went on maneuvers once. I was laying out on the deck of the USS *Shreveport*, sleeping in the sun with my shirt off. We were right in the middle of the Bermuda Triangle, but I didn't think nothing of it. I picked up the *National Enquirer* and started reading this article by Jeane Dixon. It was all the predictions about the weather and prices and stuff. And then it says, 'The USS *Shreveport* will never return. It will disappear in the Bermuda Triangle.' Right there in the paper. I tried to go back to sleep, and the whole ship started to shake, and then, boom! I heard this explosion. The loudest thing I ever heard in my life. I knew I was dead."

"Well, what happened then?"

"Oh, it was nothing. A little hot-water heater blew up or something. Everything was okay. I'll get through this, too."

Lockheed has already had a warning about absence, lateness, and appearance. And he was told by his commander that his attitude was going to get him fired. "This job is all I got left," he said. "And she's gonna ruin that, too."

Mr. Slice, when pressed to reveal the secret of his composure said, "It ain't nothing. I'm just happy to be alive and moving and still out here. Lots of people don't even last that long." He took two weeks' vacation to go fishing in Pennsylvania and was never seen or heard from again.

The Reverend Sugar Rogers, after eight vaudeville arraignments in two months, finally went to trial on a purse snatch, and demystified himself.

It was Judge Woof's first trial, and the young assistant district attorney's first trial, and the reverend's nineteenth. He represented himself and hogged the record. None of his subpoenaed big shots showed. Three months went by before the judge's sense of the right to be heard was exhausted.

On leaving the scene of the crime, Reverend Rogers had stopped at a pizzeria nearby, where he removed two books from the snatched purse, autographed them in his own name, and bestowed them on a baffled Greek lad behind the counter. The DA produced the books. Guilt beyond the shadow was proved.

Still, the black judge who presided at sentencing didn't really want to send Sugar Rogers to jail. But rather than cooperate, the defendant screamed that the conviction was unjust and that the judge was nothing but a white man's nigger. He closed his summation by running around the courtroom shouting "Nigger!" with his finger pointed at the judge, while several court officers chased him. The judge gave him 4 months in the Elmira Reformatory for all outstanding cases.

His madness took the humor away, and the claque that had followed his trial closely left, feeling jaded.

Down in AT-1, it's Big Jim, the court reporter, and me. We're the old-timers now.

11

ARREST REPORT: Alphonse Sandman. Age 44. Height, 5 foot 3. Weight, 204 pounds. Peculiarities, deformities, scars, and tattoos: heavyset. Charges, 165.15, theft of services.

He is what those in the business of law enforcement call a skell. "Skell" comes from an eighteenth-century word for rascal, now archaic except in South Africa and this system, where it is a derogatory term for people who sleep on the street. That he does, but he doesn't have the humble attitude or appearance that goes with it.

Filthy fluorescent running shoes, trimmed in hot pink, shorts of cut-off trousers held at his equator by a rope, a fringed bald head, a red nose, and a dignified smirk—Mr. Sandman stands before the court, radiating unpredictability.

LAS: Your honor, I have cautioned my client of the dangers, but he insists on representing himself.

BENCH: So long as he realizes what a serious mistake he is making. If he wants a fool for a client, that's his right.

BRIDGEMAN: You better watch it, your honor, this ain't no ordinary skell.

BENCH: Well, sir, you've insisted. Why don't you begin your defense?

D: I just wanted to wait until I was sure the boys were finished talking.

BENCH: We haven't got all day, sir.

D: Your honor, I am entitled to a United States Navy pension. For years, I have been waiting to collect my pension checks, but they refuse to send them to me because I don't have a permanent address. A Navy pension is over $200 a month, sir. And all I need is a permanent address.

BENCH: My job is only to determine bail or parole.

D: Last night, I stayed at Rikers Island, your honor. It was beautiful. Clean, nice. Wonderful people. I had my own cell, a single. The food was excellent, though I wasn't very hungry. They had a color television in the lounge. A library. What a place! So I'm asking you, please, your honor, to send me to Rikers Island. Just until I have established a permanent address there and can begin collecting my pension checks.

BENCH: Now, what's this about you going into Katz's Delicatessen last night?

D: I did.

BENCH: And did you have any money?

D: I did not.

BENCH: But you ate something there, didn't you?

D: I sure did. Three big sandwiches. And, your honor, the pastrami was so delicious it was out of this world. Even though they had me put in jail, I gotta advertise for those guys, that's how good it was.

BENCH: Then you plead guilty?

D: Yes, but—

BENCH: Time served. Next case.

D: But what about Riker's Island?

BENCH: I'm sorry, Mr. Sandman, but there are far more worthy tenants than you that I must take into consideration.

BRIDGEMAN: All right, you heard the judge. This ain't gonna be no more Holiday Inn. Find the door and step on out . . .

———

DA: Your honor, this defendant exposed himself in a residential area. We're asking for some bail.

LAS: Your honor, my client has a kidney condition and was overcome with an uncontrollable natural urge. He was relieving himself.

DA: For two blocks. That isn't relieving, that's exposing.

LAS: Relieving!

DA: Exposing.

BENCH: Paroled . . .

BENCH: Son, do you know where you are?

D: Yes, sir. I am in the colosseum.

BENCH: Counselor, I can't parole your client. He's incompetent.

LAS: But he's not violent, your honor.

BENCH: Then just think of it as a credibility problem.

LAS: Why? I trust him and I believe him.

BENCH: That's very nice, but I'm the judge.

Cops in the front row snicker. The judge smiles.

BENCH: I am.

Cops in the front row laugh. The judge jumps up, grinning. The boils on his neck light up in sequence, and he raises his arms to the crowd.

BENCH: I am the judge!

Cops in the front row cheer. The judge bows and then leans over to the snoring court reporter.

UCO: All right, knock it off. Let's have some decorum here. You guys, you know there's no eating allowed in court. Try to set an example. Officer, you heard me. Put away those potato chips.

P/O (*eating*): I'm putting them away.

BENCH: Just a psychiatric examination, Al. Don't let the record reflect any of the rest.

COURT REPORTER: What? The record? Oh, don't worry, I put everything on the record.

BENCH: Well, take it off!

———

DA: Your honor, this is a bunch of bullshit. That supposed indigent you are paroling makes more money than you and I put together and you know it.

BENCH: Counselor, you must learn to control your emotions. As a prosecutor, you cannot have these outbursts.

DA: Why not?

BENCH: Because the defendants will notice that you are a human being and not just a prosecutor.

DA: Let them.

BENCH: Then they will prey on your compassion and search for your weaknesses and forget all about the law.

DA: May I have a word with the officer on this?

BENCH: By all means.

DA: Officer, was the bar open?

A/O: What bar? It was a stationery store.

DA: It was?

A/O: I already told the whole story to two different DAs upstairs. It's all on your papers. This guy is a pimp. I know him from the neighborhood.

DA: Pimp? Then what was he doing in a stationery store?

A/O: What the hell does that matter? I was in hot pursuit.

DA: The People request a second call, your honor. This matter needs to be evaluated in greater detail.

DA: Did he make any statements, Officer?

A/O: Yeah, after readin' him his rights, he insisted it wasn't hot, so we said, Then what was a 19-inch color television doing in the shower with the curtain drawn? And he told us it was cooling off.

BENCH: The charges before me are assaulting a police officer and resisting arrest. What incident did they arise out of?

A/O: He was walking a dog without a leash.

BENCH: A dog? What kind of dog was it?

A/O: A pedigree.

BENCH: A pedigree of what breed?

A/O: All kinds.

BENCH: All kinds, Officer? Then it wasn't a pedigree, it was a mongrel.

A/O: Yes, a mongrel.

BENCH: Were you hurt, Officer?

A/O: Not really.

LAS: I'm sorry, it's late and I'm tired and I missed the statement. Could you please repeat it?

DA: Statement notice was served pursuant to Section 510.30 (IA) of the Criminal Procedure Law. Tough if you missed it, Mr. Dart, but the law does not require me to serve it twice.

LAS: Statement notice must be served on the defense. If the defense does not hear it, it hasn't been served.

DA: Statement notice was served on the record, your honor. The People are ready to proceed.

LAS: This is highly unprofessional. I believe a ruling in the ninth circuit—

BENCH: Relax, Mr. Dart. If it's on the record, the court reporter can read it back to us.

BENCH (*after pause*): Mr. Court Reporter, time is fleeting.

COURT REPORTER: What was that?

BENCH: Statement notice was just served, was it not? I'm asking you to read it back for us.

COURT REPORTER (*after long pause*): I can't make it out. We'll just have to go on.

BENCH: Sir, I order you to read us back that portion of the record where statement notice was served. We are wasting time.

COURT REPORTER: Oh, well, let me see, here . . . The defendant was absorbed . . . passing sand . . . through the purse.

BENCH: What?

COURT REPORTER: No, I got it. Was observed placing hand into the purse. Hmm . . . I can't get the next part. You see, sometimes when I fall asleep, my fingers slip down on the keys and, ah . . .

BENCH: This is getting us nowhere. I'm ordering the People to reserve statement notice immediately, under threat of contempt.

DA: Yes, your honor. In substance, the defendant admitted taking water from the complainant's purse.

BENCH: Water?

DA: Yes, sir. That's what I have in my write-up.

BENCH: How do you steal water?

DA: I don't know. Maybe it was wallet.

BENCH: Yes, wallet. That makes even better sense.

CHAPTER TEN

1

At the courthouse, just for magisterial fun, they set up barriers and for two days searched every person who came in the door. More than eight hundred knives and two guns were confiscated.

Over in the park, more bums than ever eat from the garbage of Chinese restaurants. They've even constructed a few tents out of polyethylene scraps. A Chinese brass band has started practicing there in the afternoon, right beneath the windows of AT-1. The music sounds ceremonial. I pray they are playing an Oriental "Auld Lang Syne" to the Year of the Dancing Chicken, but no such luck. Blank turnarounds get checked and counted. Data is entered, computed, and turned around. The future becomes the past.

2

When the last case before lunch was called, I put on my coat. The moment an adjournment date was set, I waved to the court reporter and bolted from the courtroom. Beating the entire audience, I ran down the hall, crossed the lobby, spun through the revolving doors, and hit the steps on the fly, just in time to see the court reporter stepping into a taxi. As it sped away, he noticed me and waved.

3

Around the globe, America is being mocked by the same little countries that used to sell it kisses. Our military threat has created a clumsy giant whose touch and technology are too heavy to rescue its pride without crushing the world. Even might doesn't make right anymore.

At home, street fairs spring up spontaneously wherever crowds gather, especially in front of the big department stores, which pressure the police to disburse them. The blocks and parks where drugs are sold have been entrenched by a fringe of old ladies hawking chuchufritas, home-fried chicken, iced tea, and chocolate.

Above the Yummy Donut Shop, a fourteen-foot-high metal sign broke from its moorings at rush hour and injured thirty-four people.

New York City shut down Sydenham Hospital, on the quiet, and was shocked when the Harlem community came out in number and marched, shouted, prayed, occupied, fought, and finally were carried away by the cops. It was the greatest organized public outpouring of Harlem anguish in over a decade, an impassioned fight to save the sacred place of birth, death, and healing, but the story soon died. That government will do its worst to someone else no longer stimulates the people who can still afford to buy the products advertised between the news.

4

The famous Decoy Program, which used to net career criminals and wanted felons, has declined, after seven years of heavy praise and publicity, to pulling in winos and double-dating teenagers on the way home from the prom with a glass of champagne in them. Not worth the danger, it's been shelved.

The new bulletproof vests, heralded by police science and public donations, turn out to be too heavy. Prolonged wearing gives the cops back problems. "And you know, if something happens and you ain't got your vest on, it gives you a funny head," they say. "Before, there was no such thing, now I'm afraid without it. I wish we never got them."

The campaign to clean up prostitution by arresting the patrons was launched with a posse of overzealous police tarts. Since all they had to put out was their badge, they hit on men so disgusting that even the whores wouldn't date them—the diseased and the 300-pounders with asymmetrical faces. It was too sad to continue, and ineffective anyway.

And I almost forgot to mention that the principal visible corruption of AT-1—police overtime—has been removed, by reform. Henceforth, prearraignment is extended. When an arrest is made, the arresting officer drops his prisoner off and goes back out on patrol. The assigned prearraignment officer, on straight time, then processes the arrest and shepherds the case through arraignment. No more overtime; consequently, there's been a drastic drop in bad arrests. So much so that the statisticians are shifting from arrests to complaints to prove that crime is up.

"Don't worry about us," say the cops cheerfully. "We'll find a way. There's always a way." Maybe they will, but intent, criminal and otherwise, doesn't fulfill what it used to.

5

One week Madison Square Garden presented The Who in concert, and night court was sprinkled with white defendants wearing The Who T-shirts. When the Sugar Hill Gang played, their T-shirts appeared under black faces. And so on, for every major New York appearance. Black audiences are respectful listeners but tear up the surrounding area on their way home. White audiences respect the neighborhood, but during the show they cut up seats, set fire to the stage, etc. The Garden is a cyclical constant.

On the other hand, bank robberies, which had fallen so low that the FBI left them to the local police, came up out of nowhere. One every few days, with full media commotion and a nickname for the evening news. The Gentleman Bandit, whose notes said "Have a nice day." The Smiling Bandit, the Priest Bandit, the Illiterate Bandit with misspelled notes, the Lady Bomber armed with a road flare, and the Disco Robber, who tried to make his getaway on roller skates with a radio wrapped around his ears.

The next week they came in ten a day. Burned-out hippies and housewives, pregnant teenagers and their boyfriends, and the bums. Their hauls plummeted: $116 vouchered, $96 vouchered, $72 vouchered. It was pitiful. And then it stopped. No pattern.

One weekend Puerto Rican nationalists bombed a washroom at the airport. On Monday the Police Department received 120 bomb threats over the telephone. On Tuesday they received 272. On Wednesday 247. On Thursday 167. On Friday 92. And on Saturday 17, which is consid-

ered normal. This happens every time, they explain. It's a
recurring cycle.

These are just examples. None of it makes sense. And
I'm supposed to be the narrator.

6

The strangers in the hall are acquaintances now. All day
long it's: How ya doing, how's your mama; how you feeling, how's your cousin? (slap). But the court part specialist
scene has dissolved.

Vaughan has grown from his tragedies to new doubts.
He's worried about his teeth or something, and pre-
occupied. He wants to lunch alone. Kitty drops by for a
visit every once in a while, but I know the rules of her culture, and the train of my thoughts should not be spoken in
front of a pregnant woman. Fortunately Kitty, too, is pre-
occupied.

The job has worn out. Too many have moved on to better things. We can't get out, so we construct a more elaborate politics. Since Vaughan, a long list of supervisors has
been tried and demoted. In fact, all the originals but Kitty
and I have had their chance.

Now that the option of being an outsider has passed, I
try to put in my time and go home and forget everything
and everybody at work. But I can't.

It is human nature to make order. When reality over-
whelms the mind, it responds with categories and cate-
gorization. And when they don't form a coherent order,
the mind just keeps on counting, trivializing the reality as
best it can.

7

The defendant is 6 foot 8, with long skinny legs and big
knees beneath checkered Bermuda shorts. He has twenty

prior arrests and twelve years of penitentiary time behind him. He wants to plead guilty to taking the two pieces of chicken valued at $1.25, but a security officer had two ribs broken in the scuffle and there is no offer.

The defendant has $1 on her and a chicken wing, claimed by the complaining witness and vouchered as the proceeds of a crime.

DA: Your honor, this defendant is a career criminal with fifteen prior arrests and numerous different names and addresses.

LAS: Your honor, would a career criminal bother with a chicken wing?

The defendant is nervous. When $500 bail is set, he unbuttons his trousers, places his genitalia on the bridge, and attempts discharge. Quickly, his presence is waived.

COURT REPORTER: Must be one of them chicken boys, I think that's what they call them. They just can't take the process. You know how it is around here.

DEPARTMENT OF CORRECTIONS (*minutes later*): We got that chicken boy handcuffed to the bars, and he's still banging his head against the wall. What should we do?

BENCH: I don't know, don't hurt him.

When Plato defined man as a featherless biped, Diogenes plucked a chicken to disprove him; who knows what we can learn from a winged thing that cannot fly but dances.

8

Two police officers are sitting in the front row. One is reading *The Eighteenth Brumaire of Louis Bonaparte* by Karl Marx. The other is not.

P/O (#2): You keep reading all the liberal shit and you're going to turn into a Communist.

P/O (#1): No, it's this job that's turning me into a Communist. That's why I have to read all this shit.

A well-groomed woman in a fur coat sits down in the front row and is told, "The front row is reserved for police officers only, please find another seat." She stands and yells, "Dr. Schwartzman killed his wife. Murdered her in her sleep in 1963. Joseph Cola and Minnie both knew about it, and he killed them too." Then she flees.

A chubby young woman approaches the rail. Her head is too big, exaggerated by the bright panels of her Burger King surplus hat. Her eyes don't focus together, and her arms end at the wrist in stumps. She asks to speak to the judge, in private, and is told to take a seat. Anywhere but the front row. She departs to the back of the courtroom, pushes her hat well down over her ears, and lets out a low nasal moan. Head bowed, she comes screaming down the aisle. At the front row, a web, of policeman's arms gathers her up and out, with hardly an interruption.

During the reign of Augustus Caesar, a Roman senator, on entering the crowded theater at Puteoli, found no one offered him a seat. By subsequent senatorial decree, at every public performance the front stalls were reserved for senators only.

A/O: She's tough. Forty-four priors for prostitution already this year, and fourteen of them had subsidiary charges of resisting arrest.

DA: Well, it's a bit more serious this time.

BRIDGEMAN: . . . Midnight Black, charged with attempted murder . . .

BENCH: What have you got to say for yourself, young lady?

D: Too bad the son-of-a-bitch didn't die.

She threw lye in a john's face. The lawyers have to confer on it. They can't agree.

BRIDGEMAN: You bad, Miss Black. One night we're gonna go out and party together.

The bridgeman gyrates to illustrate. The defendant sneers.

D: You fucking creep.

BRIDGEMAN: What's the matter, you don't like to go dancing?

D: Get out my face, motherfucker. I don't even want you looking at me.

BENCH: What's the trouble down there?

D: This creep is trying to smell my pussy.

BRIDGEMAN: All right, second call. Put your prisoner back inside, Officer. We're not calling this case again for a long while.

The cop takes his prisoner's arm. She pushes him away. He grabs her sleeve. It tears off. He throws her down and starts kicking.

DA: Oh my, not in open court.

BENCH: Officer, take her inside. Quickly.

A/O: You bitch. You fucking bitch. Now you keep me here another goddamn day. I've had all I can take from you.

Not a peep out of Midnight Black as she kicks back from the floor. Someone in the audience, presumably her man, comes flying over the wall. A court officer with a steel-filled neoprene club meets him with a knock on the head and is attacked by the man's cousin. The audience gives up a dozen young bucks to the melee, and pandemonium ensues. The lawyers huddle at the bench, safely in the center of the wagon train. The cops scramble; there are collars all over the place.

This is not what the Founding Fathers had in mind, but this is why the front row is reserved for police officers only.

9

Chickens, the front row, the lovelorn; philosophy, football, footwear. Any category in a jam.

The study of footwear distinguishes the bulky, wing-tipped brogans of lawyers on the make and the glove-soft, dainty loafers, imported from Italy, on those who have already arrived; the defendants' preference for high-topped Pro-Ked Triple Stripe basketball shoes in brown or maroon; the dark weight cops like to carry below the ankle; and the whore in gold-soled stiletto with transparent heels full of water and goldfish swimming inside.

A black market in sneakers as well as a religious service takes place on Sunday morning in the chapel of the city jail. Little guys with big feet, arrested in good sneakers, leave church in their socks.

The cruel inequities of fashion force the bums in the audience to clomp about on platform shoes with soles up to four inches thick; what once gained teenage dandies height and dash now pains and breaks bums' arches.

Every cycle has its trough. It's nothing new. In slave times, slaves wore special shoes made for them in New England factories from a mixture of sheepskin and cardboard, sold as leather. In self-defense, some slaves carved their own wooden shoes, which gave rise to a dance called the Flatfoot. One slave prayer went, "We prays for the end of tribulation, and the end of beating, and for shoes which fit our feet."

10

"You didn't happen to watch the Christopher Hour on television, did you?" Little Joe asked.

I never even heard of it.

"It's on Sunday morning at eight o'clock. I guess not many people look at it. Too bad. I was the guest star last week."

I wished I had seen it.

"For being a good samaritan, you know. But never mind that, come into the clerk's office. I've got something I want to show you."

I followed him in. He unpacked his shopping bag and took out a clean new copy of *Variety*, "Newspaper of the Theater Arts." Inside it, a small box read: *In my lifetime, I have collected and summarized over 800 stories, suitable for novels, films, and television plays. Interested parties contact Joseph L. Dunnay, Brownsville, Brooklyn.*

"Howard, you know I have never received any payment or other remuneration for all the good work I have done in my life, other than in my heart."

I knew.

"But I'm hoping to get some interesting replies."

He put the paper away and sat down. "You'll want a pencil and paper for this," he said and began at breakneck speed.

"In 1940, Bertram Campbell, a prosperous stockbroker, was arrested, out of the blue, for passing a bad check. For $10,000. At the lineup he was positively identified by the woman from American Express who had cashed the check. 'But I'm innocent,' he insisted. Nobody believed him. He was convicted of forgery on her testimony and sentenced to 10 to 15 years. After a short time his wife ran out of money. She sold their possessions, then their house, and moved to Queens Village."

Joe burst into tears for a moment and drew his first decent-sized breath. "Alone in Queens Village, she had nothing.

"After Bertram Campbell served three and a half years, a man called Alexander Thiel confessed to the crime. Bertram Campbell was released and told to stay away from Wall Street. His case was investigated by the Bar Association, up on Forty-fourth Street. They asked the police, the detectives, the DA, the judge—they asked them, 'How could you be so sure? How could you be so harsh? Why wasn't this man given probation or something like that?' But there were no answers.

"Bertram Campbell got a job with a fuel oil company in Elmhurst, Queens. Governor Dewey awarded him $100,-000 compensation and $25,000 for his wife. Six months later, Bertram Campbell died."

Joe wept a bit more, blew his nose, and carried on.

"January 1, New Year's Day, 1929. Police Officer William Lundy interrupted a speakeasy holdup and was shot dead. There was a public outcry. A dragnet on the area came up with all the bums and drunks. One of them confessed under duress. He got 99 years to life. His wife divorced him and took their children to California. Nobody remembered him but his mother, who believed he was innocent.

"She took a job scrubbing floors for $20 a week. She saved half of it, and lived on $10 a week. She lived on nothing but the hope of saving her son.

"After ten years of scrubbing floors, she put an ad in the paper offering $5,000 reward for any additional evidence in her son's case. You see, $10 every week makes $500 a year, and after ten years, she had $5,000. A young newspaperman named James McClure, of the *Chicago Times*, saw her ad and became interested. He found the real murderer, who confessed. The woman's son was freed. I forgot his name. He only got $2,500 in compensation.

"What's the trouble, son? Don't you want to write any of this down?"

11

*It's almost closing time. Only three cases are left on the
bridge. But they all belong to Mr. Dart, all potential trouble. And Judge Woof, suffering from sciatica, is sitting.*

BENCH: Sir, why do you want to address the court? You
have a superior attorney standing beside you, provided by
the state for just that purpose. You can avoid all kinds of
problems by allowing him to represent you.

D: No. I must speak.

BENCH: Very well, but I must caution you not to discuss
the merits of the case, and to remember everything you say
is on the record and may be used against you.

D: I speak the truth. The truth cannot hurt me.

BENCH: I'm sure you don't know what you're doing, but go
ahead.

D: Your honor. You set this $2,000 bail because you don't
understand. This thing that happened is nothing. I pick up
this woman in my taxi. Maybe she is a prostitute, I don't
know. She give me what you people call oral sex, and I
give her $20. I show her this gun. It doesn't work. If the
gun worked, I wouldn't be alive today. A fare pulled it on
me and shot it twice. Nothing happened, and I took it off
him. If the gun worked, I'd be dead.

When I show this gun to the woman, she bug out. She's
all smoked up with reefer. She run out the taxi and got a
cop. That's all . . .

BENCH: All right, Officer, lodge him.

D: I told the truth.

LAS: Yeah, but you connected yourself to the gun on the
record. I could have got you off. The prostitute wouldn't
come in and testify. They had nothing on you until you
opened your mouth.

DA (*laughing*): That dope just made our case. I'm ordering

the record of this arraignment. How soon can I have it?

COURT REPORTER: Uh huh.

BENCH: Have we set a date?

LAS: I hope you're satisifed, you've totally destroyed my defense.

But Mr. Dart never took it out on his clients, and the next case was already called in.

BRIDGEMAN: Docket Number Y021040, Alvin Cummerbund, charged with 220.31, possession of a controlled substance in the sixth degree on the complaint of Officer Puddle, Transit.

WRITE-UP: 5 Tuinals offered to an off-duty cop for $3.50 each. D has Tuinal prescription.

LAS: Your honor, this looks like a setup to me. If this is an undercover sale, why didn't currency change hands? Why isn't there vouchered money? Instead, all we have is word against word. Furthermore, this incident occurred in front of my client's house.

DA: We're asking for some bail. This defendant has a long and serious record: twenty-four priors, and his last arrest was for homicide.

LAS: It was not a homicide! It was a fight with a transit policeman, in which my client was badly beaten. As a result, those charges were dismissed and a lawsuit was filed against the Police Department, still pending. And it forces me to ask what an off-duty transit cop was doing in front of my client's house, if not to harass him because of this suit.

BENCH: Bail is set in the amount of $100 bond or $75 cash. Shall we set it down for Tuesday?

LAS: Just a minute, your honor. Didn't you hear me? This is a setup, and you're playing right into their hands.

BENCH: I heard you, Counselor, and took note of what you said in making my decision.

D: Your honor, me and the officer was just rapping. I never give him anything. I never sold him nothing. I have a prescription for those pills. They are medication. This is wrong.

BENCH: Tuesday.

LAS: I have the prescription right here. All you have is the word of this cop.

BENCH: I wish someone would let me run this place for a change. Mr. Bridgeman, stamp up the papers and let's get going.

LAS: Your honor, my client is a black man. A poor black man.

BENCH: Mr. Dart—

LAS: If he were not poor and black he would be walking out of here, paroled. But since he is, $75 is tantamount to a remand. He couldn't make seventy-five cents.

BENCH: That's enough.

LAS: I'm making a record, your honor.

BENCH: You've made your record. And we've moved on.

LAS: Of course. We can't waste time on a poor black man. Who cares what we do to him, he doesn't count.

BENCH: This case is finished, Mr. Dart, and you are bordering on contempt.

LAS: This case is not finished!

BENCH: Officers, remove him!

The delighted court crew leaps at Mr. Dart. An elbow under his chin, and feet aloft, Mr. Dart struggles, and a barrage of garbled "furthermores" rolls out. Alvin Cummerbund goes off to jail, and the last case of the day is addressed.

BRIDGEMAN: Hey, where are you going with that attorney? The instant case is his.

BENCH: All right, bring him back. This last case is such a simple matter, it isn't fair to hold it over. Let's just finish up and go home.

DA: Your honor, the People consent to parole on this case.

BENCH: Paroled on consent of the People. Give us a one-month date, sir, and we can all get out of here.

BRIDGEMAN: Wait a minute, I haven't even called the case into the record yet.

COURT REPORTER: Yes, you have, I put the whole thing down already.

BRIDGEMAN: This court stands adjourned.

The judge took off his robe. Mr. Dart dusted off his ego, put on his coat, and calmly apologized to the judge, who shook hands with him and smiled. I was disappointed.

The following week, the judge was rotated from arraignments to an all-purpose part upstairs. Mr. Dart appeared before him, was cited for contempt and fined $250.

Contempt citations are rare in Criminal Court. He must have said something really bad to get one, but it was not dramatic. Contempt is a summary proceedings. Once cited, there is no argument, and none was allowed. Mr. Dart couldn't even plead for an adjournment. The fine machines was already locked up, so they had to give it to him.

During the week of Mr. Dart's parole, the grapevine was silent, and the Legal Aid Society refused to appear before Judge Woof. With his calendars emptied, his disposition rate plunged. The Officer of Court Administration had another nuisance to deal with, and the judge had back pains.

The scene at sentencing was reputedly damp. A big chief from the Legal Aid Society made a speech about the meaning of the bar and a license to practice law in this state. How this action would blemish the record and jeopardize the livelihood of poor Mr. Dart.

Mr. Dart followed with a long apology and even bleaker picture of his future, after this case. Then he wrote a check.

The Legal Aid Society went back to work. Judge Woof was transferred to Brooklyn. And the court part personnel went back to hating Mr. Dart and waiting for his crack-up.

He's such a powerful presence that they can hate him instead of hating the system and themselves in it. It is for all of us that Mr. Dart faces destruction.

Grateful, I give him the big hello that Little Joe taught me to give everyone. It annoys him.

12

CW: You see, the television don't work properly. You need a pliers to change the channel, play with the aerial, it isn't easy. I told the boy not to change the program. Me and his mother was watching the movie. When I got back with the wine, the ball game was on.
DA: And did there come a time when you quarreled?
CW: We've had many differences, verbal and otherwise, in the past. And he owed me a dollar, too.
DA: But what happened in this incident?
CW: He come at me with the pliers ...

CW: How long do I know him? I remember the day he was born ... When did I first see the knife? When he stabbed me with it.
BENCH: Do you mean you saw the blade as it went into your stomach?
CW: No, I saw the blood gush out, and I knew.
BENCH: And then what did he do?
CW: He cut my arm and neck and took my wallet.
BENCH: And what did you do?
CW: I walked to the hospital.

CROSS-COMPLAINT: Housewives fight. One rock, four inches across, in a sock; one mop and pail, vouchered.

ARREST REPORT: Peculiarities, deformities, scars, and tattoos: right arm, beautiful spread eagle in red and blue over

King of Darkness; left arm, the word *praxis*, with the letter
X an enlarged religious cross, done in the jailhouse style.
CHARGES: Assault in the second degree and criminal pos-
session of a weapon.
WRITE-UP: Fight under theater marquee. D hit CW with
the letters *G* and *T*.

*D slashes girlfriend's throat. He had promised her $25 for
the electric bill, but bought a TV set instead. She was trying
to take it back when he killed her.*

*D beats wife and leaves. She calls precinct. D returns,
breaks down door, and beats her again, with a stick, until
the cops arrive. Welts on her arms and legs. Head broken
open in three places. CW declines prosecution. Claims she
hit her head on a cabinet and fell down.*

WRITE-UP: D kicks in barred window. She falls in and can't
be reached. Across roof are footprints of two shoes coming
and one shoe leaving. Recovered shoe matches the one D
wearing. Both shoes vouchered.
  *The defendant is forty-five years old, tall, fat, and pow-
erful. As big as a refrigerator, but wearing only a T-shirt
and pants. In addition to no shoes, he has no name and address and no money. And not having entered the premises,
he doesn't even have a burglary charge.*
  *He pleads to criminal trespass and signs the conditional
discharge, but he won't leave. The crew, led by Big Jim,
wearing gray work gloves, drag him out.*
CPS: How the hell can you throw that guy out? It's cold,
and all he has on is a T-shirt.
UCO: What else can I do? I never went to college.
CPS: But the guy has no shoes.
  *Big Jim looks down at his own shoes, suddenly accused
of having them.*
UCO: Is that supposed to be my fault?

13

The boredom begins with the first shiver of withdrawal and matures until there is no reality but that of your own wait. Boredom is part of the sadism, part of the mask.

My mask is solid. Rapping in the halls, sleeping in the judicial library, or shooting pinball at Maruffi's bar, while the rest of the white suckers work their butts off. I'm so cool, I'm automatic.

It's after work that I feel soiled by the work of divining souls and feeding them to the devil as a hundred new names for his infinite work.

I can't see anymore. I can't record, and I can't stop. And I have come to a sad respect for the heartless intelligence of the Prosecutor's Management Information System (PROMIS), whose computers don't expect to make sense or understand and, therefore, only count.

14

First thing Monday morning, Vaughan pulled me aside at the clock. "There's something I've got to tell you, and . . . um . . . I thought I should be the one to tell you first. Al Taylor passed away. Last Saturday night. They say he was found in the street. They say it was drugs."

"What happened?"

"I don't know. That's as much as I heard. How it happened really doesn't matter. It happened."

"It does," I said.

"Well, you know how death is. It doesn't need a reason."

The word in AT-1 was the same. Died in the street of an overdose, and no one knew any more than that. In AT-1, they never say drugs, they say fluthenazine, phencyclidine, ethchlorovinol or smack. But in this case, all they knew was drugs.

By midmorning, the notices were up along the bank of elevators: Albert Taylor, Criminal Court reporter, died on Saturday. Viewing will be Wednesday, services will be on Thursday. Ortiz Funeral Home.

At the funeral I recognized his father and four brothers by family resemblance. His wife and ten-year-old son, both white, he had never mentioned. Most of the mourners were women. Court reporters, Legal Aid attorneys, and figures from his stories.

I went up and looked at the body. It was dressed in a fifteen-year-old square suit with a necktie tight around the neck, which he could never stand. Without the nervous energy and hyperanimation, it wasn't him. The expression was all wrong. Maybe it was a wax model.

A preacher gave a brief biography, mainly for the family. He dwelled on the voted-most-likely-to-succeed high school track star, and his naval career. The last sixteen years of his life were reduced to: "And he worked as a reporter in Criminal Court." Everyone at work said there was lots of singing at black funerals, but all we got was "Swing Low, Sweet Chariot" at the beginning, and "Rock of Ages" at the end, done solo.

I bumped into Big Jim on the way out, surprised that I had missed him. Underneath his motorcycle parka was an ancient suit, a yellowed shirt, and a wrinkled slim-jim tie. I wanted to walk back to the courthouse alone, but he asked me to wait for the bus with him.

At the bus stop, two hookers were propositioning all passers, including us. It seemed strange on a quiet street at ten-thirty in the morning. We waited without speaking.

After a while I followed him into the Jewish delicatessen across the street and had a beer at his suggestion. It was ice cold and made me shiver. I left half of it, and we went back.

When the bus came, I got on and put my money in the box and Big Jim showed his court officer's badge. The bus driver slammed on the brakes and yelled, "No badges."

"Since when," said Big Jim, tense and insulted.

"Since a long time ago," said the bus driver. "This bus ain't moving until you pay your fare."

Big Jim drew a deep breath of self-control and muttered something to himself. "I guess I'll see you at work, I'm gonna walk back," he said, and got off the bus. It was the longest conversation we had all morning.

Back in AT-1, a pleasant young woman was taking down the record, just as if it were one of Al's frequent absences. There was no mention of the funeral or the deceased until later in the day, when Big Jim said, "Yeah, he could be a real pain in the ass, but he was something special."

Did the court reporter kill himself, or was he just dead-ended by life? Did whatever set him free finally lock him out? And dare we ask such questions of a life?

AUTOPSY REPORT: Albert Taylor, black male, approximately forty-three years old, measuring 5 feet 10 inches in body length and weighing 150 pounds. The scalp is covered with abundant black and kinky hair in disarray manner and mingling with a few strands of white hair . . . The teeth appear in good condition . . . The neck is not remarkable . . . Scar needle marks are noted along the vent of the left leg in its antero-medial aspect. Multiple hyperpigmented scarred needle marks are noted along the ventral of both extremities and fresh needle marks are noted in the lower middle third of the left forearm and the lower third of the right arm.

CAUSE OF DEATH: Acute and chronic intravenous narcotism.

CHEMICAL EXAMINATION: Death from acute mixed drugs (lidocaine, cocaine, and propoxyphene) intoxication.

Lidocaine is a synthetic cocaine, and propoxyphene is the tranquilizer Darvon. His own special concoction, a cocktail mixer to the end.

He was found by his wife, at home, in bed, face down with a nosebleed, at eleven o'clock at night. He had a history of moderate intake of alcohol and involvement with drugs for less than a year. His only recorded medical history was severe headaches for the last year.

Who we are, what we want, or why we inhabit this earth doesn't really show.

CHAPTER ELEVEN

1

CPS: How's things?

LAS: Oh, so-so. I got a letter from one of my clients the other day. Ella Galopcyznyzsky.

CPS: Oh, really. How is she?

LAS: She's fine. You know, Nelson Rockefeller was her FBI contact, and she loved him and was very upset when he died. But it's all working out. The FBI have reassigned her to David Bowie, and she's very pleased with him, even if he is a rock star. She's sure her mother will just adore David. And she's just come back from another 730 examination, found fit, of course . . .

2

With the passage of time and vigorous scrubbing, the messages on the toilet walls gradually change: *My kids need me, not O.T. The World Sucks. A policeman died to save my brother, pray for all policemen. Albino pink motherfucker, go back to your caves of Europe* has faded to a transparent Garveyite reference, obscured by *Whitey sucks black dick.*

In the stall, a primitive mural, in the conventions of archaic perspective and diagram, depicts the judge, the lawyer, and the nigger, with sexual organs indicating the flow of power. It is captioned, *I accept you I deny you.*

And shining through it all is the indelible *Officer Culley (TPF) is a low-life scum bag, I hope he drops dead.* He did, in the line of duty, a few months ago.

Tommy, AT-1's most dapper, punctual, and dedicated bum, was held up at gunpoint in the toilet. He lost his hat and wallet, which he really didn't care about, and the deed to his burial plot, which was the only thing in the world he cared about. And the knobs have disappeared from the sink in the judges' bathroom.

D: I know all about this kind of thing, your honor, but I'm against the whole system. I once spent five years in Iola Sanitorium for refusing to wear shoes. Finally, I put the shoes on and they let me go. So I understand, but I can't believe in a system that defecates on water. Water is for blessings and washing and growing things, not shit . . .

3

In the halls, I'm always running into the dead. Officer Culley, Bob Bilodeau, Shimano, and other cops I know only by sight. Sometimes I've got the wrong guy, or the bullet just grazed them and the rumors were highly exaggerated. Sometimes they are alive, but shot somebody else, off-duty, and are in the system as defendants. But usually, they really are dead. If I try to walk right up and shake their hand, they change into somebody else.

When the eighty-two-year-old man arrested for sexually molesting a seven-year-old girl died of a heart attack in the middle of his arraignment, I had to check off the dismissal coded DD on my turnaround document. Abated by death of defendant. The only other time I did that was for the guy who slashed his wrist with a razor blade on the prisoner's bench.

Them, I never saw again. Or the court reporter.

4

Al Taylor's death notice was replaced by one that read: *Two reels of evidence were stolen from a Uher tape recorder in Room 600. Anyone with any information, please call Room 600.*

Everyone smiled at the note because they knew who did it, but no one ever called. What the master sees as valuable evidence in a criminal case, his field hands see as blank cassettes. This really is a plantation.

5

Lockheed got fired, just after his wife asked for a divorce. The poverty that followed brought them back together, and left them devoted lovers and parents. He turned up recently looking settled and content in a classic tweed suit. Same work clothes as a prospering lawyer, but he's a hotel security guard. Midnight to eight in the morning, Monday and Tuesday off. The money is less, too.

Kitty gave birth to a baby girl, just as beautiful as she had planned, but hasn't returned to work. At the beginning of every month, she calls in to say she can't find a baby-sitter, and extends her leave.

Little Joe got no replies to his expensive advertisement and, for a chance of pace, is away doing volunteer work at the Jewish Home for the Aged in Far Rockaway.

Big Jim was in a motorcycle accident and broke his shades. He now comes to work in ordinary transparent spectacles. His eyes are soft and slightly shy. The new look has cost him his mystery. And there is a new tension between him and his staff.

"Now, they call me the Idi Amin of AT-1," he told me.

"Whatever for?" I replied.

"Probably for being a ruthless, sadistic, cruel, and brutal dictator," he whispered.

Judge Woof has returned from Brooklyn. His back is much improved. Still in love with the law, still determined to be beholden to nothing but a sense of justice, but not so cheerful as before. It's a different phase of his judicial career.

Mr. Dart was offered a job on the faculty of a prestigious East Coast law school, and he accepted it, instead of having his scheduled nervous breakdown.

I'm coming into court in brand-new Triple Stripe felony shoes and no one even notices. Last year, when I wore sneaks, the Office of the District Attorney put out a special memo on dress code mentioning it, and peer pressure made me stop. Now everybody's gone and I'm acceptable. There is only Vaughan to tell me that at a certain age you've got to act like a man and leave your gym shoes in the gym.

It's an empty gesture. We're both stagnating. Vaughan switched from the tabloid to *The New York Times,* and now reads the sports section last instead of first. Recently I caught him deeply engrossed in a book called *Origins of World War I, 1870–1914.* He said he found it in the judges' chambers, and as long as it got him through to five o'clock he didn't care what it said.

The bums alone maintain the continuity. They are proof of public access, humble before the law, and thrilled when anyone in a uniform or a clean suit pays attention to them. When I ask them why they come to court, they won't say. And when I ask them if they find it interesting, they give me a dirty look.

6

Late one morning, an eleven-year-old girl complainant testified to her rape, and I thought about my lunch. She told how she went out with her father's best friend to get some beer, and he took her to the playground, and he took her to the shed, and he took off her pants and he took off his pants, and he put it in here. Nervous, she slipped into Spanish, then a whisper that the judge complained he couldn't hear. Then she went rigid and had to be taken off the stand, and I decided I was tired of Chinese food and would try the Mexican place. And then I knew I had to go.

"It's easy to get depressed and not even know it," said Vaughan when I told him. "You go around with your whole life falling down, telling yourself everything is okay. And you believe it, and hang on to it, bad as it is, because—it seems like, even in your own feelings, there's always security at the top and bottom, and everything in between is a risk. You don't take risks when you're depressed. That's the deal here."

And then he walked into personnel, on impulse, and resigned. He told some people that he was going to a job as a Toyota salesman in Virginia. They congratulated him and wished him well. He told others that he was going to Africa. They didn't believe him.

"After all the time I'm working here, they believe I could be some goddamn Toyota salesman. They never even found out who I am. No wonder I don't know anymore."

Anyway, Vaughan went to Virginia with no definite plans, and I felt as if someone had put glue on my chair.

7

AT-1 is still trying. A dedicated senior clerk gave a maintenance engineer $10 of his own money to fix the light over the clerk's desk. So now a note saying *Out of order. Needs ballast* flutters from the blinking fixture.

The filthy old flag has been replaced by a new one, edged in gold fringe and wrapped in plastic, just like the old flag before I came. Dirt has already collected on the plastic and awaits the next rinse cycle of reform.

There is a new velvet rope on the gate, and the doorknob to the pens doesn't fall off anymore. Last time it did, in the middle of night court, a group of cops imbued with Yankee ingenuity averted a critical pileup by replacing it with a bent coat hanger and a ball of masking tape. And it has lasted.

Pursuant to the famous theory of gravity, the big hand on the clock has slowly made its way downward, almost to eight-thirty. A progress of eight minutes over the last two years. And believe me, every eight minutes of sitting here feels like two years.

8

The common law comes from sanctioned customs; customs so ancient that man's memory runneth not to the contrary. Since ever, forever, and ay, people have been coming to court with a notion of justice and an expectation to receive it, or a notion of the system and how to exploit it. And what they've always received instead is an explanation and a demonstration of where the power lies.

But after all the millenniums since the advent of collective memory, you don't judge the courts by how they serve the society; you judge the society by whom it brings to court. And you don't judge corruption by the exercise of power and rule but by the habit of obedience to a power believed illegitimate and a rule considered usurped.

9

"Violent crime rose by 17 percent in all categories," says the FBI Uniform Crime Index. "Home safe," say the cops after night court, with a look more of warning than farewell.

What is the hope for such a broad society in so small a place, where the rich and powerful congregate in full view of the oppressed indigent? What is the hope when the many feel inadequate and inferior, and the millions at the bottom live lives that often fall below the natural dignity of human nature?

None of us feels we belong here or deserve this.

So, cognizant of the rate of achievement of justice in the law of rule and procedure rather than the whim of tyrants; recognizing obedience to the common law as the measure of civilization, without which, after some unimportant violence, we would all be dead; and understanding that the system as I know it represents the pinnacle of democratic impulse, where more rights and protections are extended more broadly and more bravely than ever before—

Evaluating the limousines and skyscrapers versus the tired feet, chronic no heat and smashed plumbing; assessing the higher technology and lower community; appraising the social contract versus people so traumatized that they have been disenfranchised from their ability to think—the whole thing stinks.

What's best has passed. We all know it. America isn't growing anymore. That dream, that success, that destiny no longer molds the mask. From the privilege of my position, invisibility is no longer necessary. The pain of being here has lost its meaning. The whole thing stinks, I quit.

10

If you ever get arrested, give your name and address and the date and place of your birth—nothing else. All you say is that you want to see a lawyer. Insist on three phone calls. You have the right to them, but only if you insist. Unless you are a person of means, with hereditary or political connections to power, you will probably want to consent to fingerprinting. You may refuse, but then they may want to step on your fingers.

Until you see a lawyer, don't discuss the case with anyone. When pushed, just maintain your innocence. Even if they show you videotapes of yourself committing the crime, you don't have to admit it. Make them prove it at trial. That is the system.

If you know beforehand of your impending arrest, wash, go to the toilet, and get plenty of sleep. Or be unconscious. And don't have any dice, drugs, or weapons on your person.

Trust what they tell you unless you have a choice. And trust your lawyers, even if they're free. Winning is very important to lawyers, however it appears. If your lawyer is dumb, then you are stuck and no advice applies. Lawyers are the part of the system that represents your interest. You are there not to like them but to help them.

And always remember that you are in somebody else's store. They make the rules. They own the muscle. Be patient. Be philosophical.